P9-BTN-093

When Can I Start Dating?

Questions about Love, Sex, and a Cure for Zits

JAMES N. WATKINS

THE WHY FILES

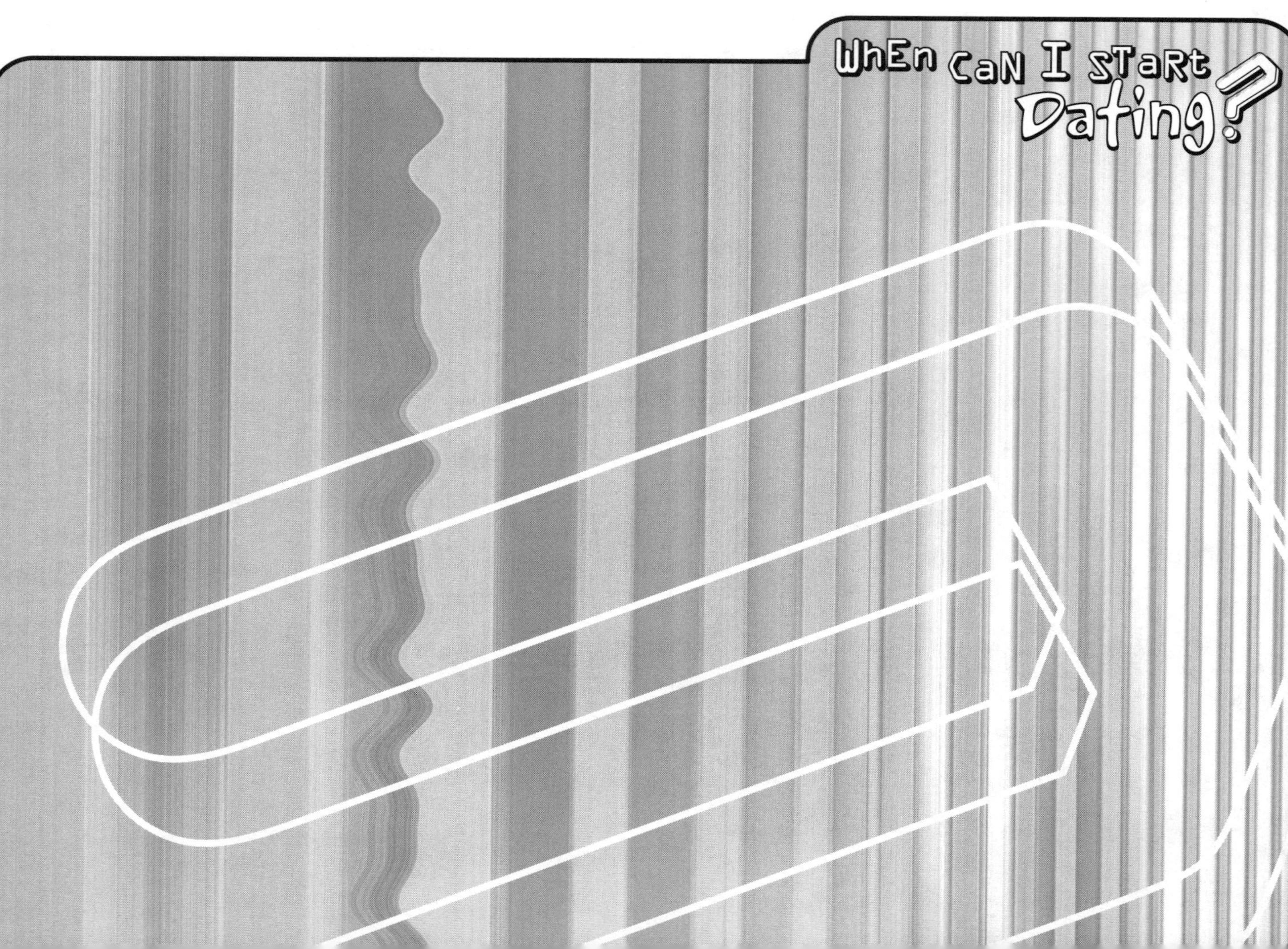
WhEn CaN I sTaRt
Dating?

QuESTIoNS about Love, Sex, and a Cure for Zits

JAMES N. WATKINS

CPH
SAINT LOUIS

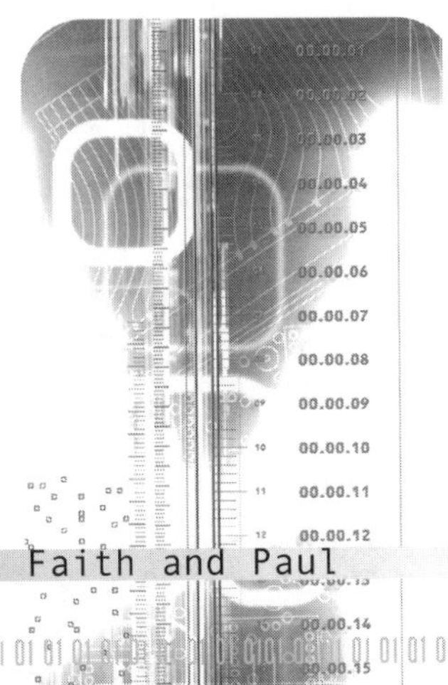

To my two favorite young people, Faith and Paul

01 01 01 01 01 01 01 01 01 0101 01 01 01 01 01 01 01 01 01 01 01 0101 01 01 01 01 01 01 01 01 01 0101 01 01 01 01 01 01 01 01 01 01 0101 01 01

LIBRARY
FRANKLIN PIERCE COLLEGE
RINDGE, NH 03461

The Why Files

When Can I Start Dating?
Questions about Love, Sex, and a Cure for Zits

Is There Really Life after Death?
Questions about School Shootings, Grief, and Coming Back as a Gerbil

Are There Really Ghosts?
Questions about Angels, the Supernatural, and the Psychic Friends Network

Unless otherwise indicated, Scripture quotations are taken from the HOLY BIBLE, NEW INTERNATIONAL VERSION®. NIV®. Copyright © 1973, 1978, 1984 by International Bible Society. Used by permission of Zondervan Publishing House. All rights reserved.

Scripture quotations marked TLB are from The Living Bible copyright © 1971 by Tyndale House Publishers, Wheaton, Illinois. All rights reserved.

Scripture quotations marked NRSV are taken from the New Revised Standard Version Bible, copyright ©1989, Division of Christian Education of the National Council of the Churches of Christ in the United States of America. Used by permission. All rights reserved.

Cover design by Karol Bergdolt. Interior design by Tamara Clerkley.

Parts of this book are adapted from *The World's Worst Date* copyright © 1985 by James N. Watkins, *The Teen Sex Survival Manual* © 1987 by James N. Watkins published by Bridge Publishing, and *Sex Is Not a Four-Letter Word* © 1991 by James N. Watkins published by Tyndale House Publishers.

Copyright © 1985, 1987, 1991, 2000 James N. Watkins
Published by Concordia Publishing House
3558 S. Jefferson Avenue, St. Louis, MO 63118-3968
Manufactured in the United States of America

Individuals who purchase this product may reproduce the list on page 30 and the "Thinking about Yourself" list on page 59 for personal use only. All rights reserved.
Except as noted above, no part of this publication may be reproduced, stored in a retrieval system, or transmitted, in any form or by any means, electronic, mechanical, photocopying, recording, or otherwise, without the prior written permission of Concordia Publishing House.

Library of Congress Cataloging-in-Publication Data

Watkins, James, 1952-

The why files : when can I start dating? : questions about love, sex, and a cure for zits / Jim Watkins.
p. cm.
ISBN 0-570-05249-1 (alk. paper)
1. Teenagers--Sexual behavior--Miscellanea. 2. Sexual ethics for teenagers--Miscellanea. 3. Dating (Social customs)--Miscellanea. 4. Sex instruction for teenagers--Miscellanea. I. Title.
HQ27 .W363 2000
305. 235--dc21

00-008575

1 2 3 4 5 6 7 8 9 10 09 08 07 06 05 04 03 02 01 00

CONTENTS

Foreword

Forewords are usually a big, fat waste of time. Nobody reads them. They're often just some fairly famous person saying a few nice things about a book by a slightly less famous person.

Well, that's just not the case with this foreword. I'm not famous. Neither is Jim Watkins, the author of this book—at least not yet. (He's hoping you'll tell 10 million of your closest friends about him, then they'll tell 10 million of their closest friends, and ... well, you get the idea.) So this foreword is different.

And, while nobody reads forewords, everybody likes a good Top Ten list, right? So with that in mind, here are the Top Ten Reasons to Read *When Can I Start Dating?* by Jim Watkins:

10. He's still pretty much an adolescent himself, so he knows what he's talking about.
9. When you discover how totally whacked-out he is, your problems and insecurities will seem small by comparison.
8. He can use the word **phenylthylamine** and the phrase "dead-fish breath" in the same book.
7. He knows about guys (he is one, more or less).
6. He knows about girls (he lived in a girls' dorm for 6 years ... but you'll have to read the book to hear about that!).
5. He knows about parents (he has two of his own).
4. He knows about kids (he has two of his own).
3. He knows about dates (he had two of his own ... okay, maybe more, but it depends on whose stories you believe).
2. He's helped millions of kids with their problems and written billions of books and articles for teens and young adults (give or take a few).

And the number one reason to read ***When Can I Start Dating?*** by Jim **Watkins:**

1. He needs the money from the sales of this book to buy my books!

Bob Hostetler

Acknowledgments

Thanks to 1,000 teens from northern Indiana for their honest questions.

Thanks to Andrea Basinger for her keyboarding skills.

Thanks to Stephanie Troyer, an award-winning author at just 16, for providing invaluable input as a critic of the rough draft.

And thanks to Rachel Hoyer of Concordia Publishing House and my agent, Janet Kobobel Grant, for their encouragement and editorial skills.

You made me look good!

Introduction to The Why Files

Jim: Excuse me. I'm taking a survey. Could you answer a few questions?

Jim: Sure, that sounds kind of interesting ... wait a minute! You can't interview me—I'm you ... I mean, you're me!

Jim: Look, Jim, I'm just doing my job.

Jim: You can't interview you, I'm me, I mean, you're me ...

Jim: Just look in the mirror and answer my first question: What do you think is the number one issue on the minds of young people today?

Jim: This is ridiculous!

Jim: Just answer the question.

Jim: Okay, fine. I just finished surveying more than 1,000 junior and senior high students on three subjects: adolescence, death, and the supernatural. I distributed the surveys in public and private schools, in rural as well as urban ...

Jim: Okay, okay, so you surveyed a bunch of people. Just answer the question: What is the number one issue on the minds of young people today?

Jim: Dating issues were the most asked questions on the adolescence survey, "Is there really life after death?" topped the death survey, and questions about God and ghosts topped our supernatural survey.

Jim: So how did you pick these three topics?

Jim: While I was editor of a teen magazine, I kept looking for articles on love and sexuality, but I never found any that honestly dealt with the issues, so I started writing them myself. Those articles eventually turned into three books on sex—everything from abortion to zits!

Then my book editor asked me to write about death, which, surprisingly, our surveys showed was of even more interest to young people than sex! So I've covered everything from grief to out-of-body experiences.

Finally, after you've spent 10 years writing about sex and death, the only bigger subject is the universe itself: God and the whole supernatural realm of angels, demons, ghosts, psychic powers, etc., etc.

Jim: And what makes you think you have the answers to all those questions?

Jim: Well, I've worked as an author and youth speaker all my professional life, and I lived in a girls' dorm for six years, and ...

Jim: You lived in a girls' dorm?!

Jim: I knew interviewing myself was a bad idea!

Jim: So?

Jim: My wife was resident director at Indiana Wesleyan University while I worked with students on campus. What I was trying to say is that I've learned as much working with teens and young people as they've ever learned from me. And one of the most important lessons I've learned is that simple answers to complex questions don't satisfy young people.

Jim: So you don't have a lot of answers?

Jim: Well, I've tried to take young people and their questions seriously, plus I've done an awful lot of research to find the answers.

Jim: So you *do* have all the answers?

Jim: No! I don't have all the answers, but I try to share some thoughts that will help young people think about these three big subjects. I realize that each person is different, so it's hard to give an answer that satisfies everyone. That's why I try to give a general answer when young people write or e-mail questions. But I usually close with something like this:

> ***I'm glad my writing has helped you deal with some of these issues, but paper and ink are not enough. I wish I could sit down and talk with you face-to-face over a***

Diet Pepsi. Books, articles, letters, and websites can be helpful, but those can't address your one-of-a-kind situation.

You need a real, live, flesh-and-blood person to give you emotional, social, and spiritual support as well as guidance to make the right choices. I'd encourage you to talk to an adult you trust, such as a member of the clergy, a school counselor, or a youth worker.

Jim: So if your readers want to get in touch with you, how do they do that?

Jim: I love to hear from readers! They can write me c/o Concordia Publishing House, Book Development Department, 3558 South Jefferson Avenue, St. Louis, MO 63118-3968 or e-mail me at whyfiles@jameswatkins.com.

We've also set up a website with links to the resources mentioned in this book series. There are additional resources and up-to-the-minute information on sex, death, and the supernatural at www.jameswatkins.com.

Jim: Anything else in closing?

Jim: I'd like to thank each reader for buying this book. I hope the time we spend together through these pages will be not only informative, but encouraging as well. And, of course, I'd love them to tell all their friends about these three books. Or, better yet, buy a copy of all three books for all of their friends!

Jim: Well, thanks for your time. I'll let you get back to your writing.

Jim: You're welcome ... I think.

Introduction

I have in my right hand, direct from my home office, today's Top Ten list: What are the top 10 questions teens ask about love and sexuality?

10. What is sex all about?
9. When is intercourse okay?
8. What is happening to my body?
7. What should you do on a date?
6. Why is there so much pressure to have sex?
5. Why does love hurt so much?
4. When will puberty start? (Fifty-six young people asked this question. Eleven, however, wanted to know "When will it stop?")
3. Why are guys always thinking about sex?
2. How can I know if I'm really in love?

And the number one response when we asked nearly 1,000 junior and senior high students, "What's a question you have about love and sexuality?"

1. When can I start dating?

As I mentioned in the introduction to the series, I don't have all the answers. For those, you'll need to talk to the sixth-grade guy who wrote "I know it all" on his survey. However, I was a teen for seven years, have a 17-year-old son at home, and have worked with teens for more than 20 years.

I've tried to take your questions seriously and have carefully researched for medically and morally sound answers. (I think I've learned more about tampons than I, as a guy, want to know!) And I've never been known to duck any tough questions, so we'll deal with the usual questions addressed by youth leaders and teachers as well as some of the tougher ones on masturbation, oral sex, and homosexual behaviors.

You may want to think of this book as a buffet. You don't have to read it in order from chapter 1 through the endnotes. Sample the questions you're dealing with at this point in your life, then come back to others when you're ready. Enjoy!

> Dear friend, I pray that you may enjoy good health and that all may go well with you, even as your soul is getting along well. (3 John 2)

Jim Watkins

00.00.01
00.00.02
00.00.03
00.00.04
00.00.05
00.00.06
00.00.07
00.00.08
00.00.09
00.00.10
00.00.11
00.00.12
00.00.13
00.00.14
00.00.15
00.00.16
00.00.18
00.00.19
00.00.20
00.00.21
00.00.22
00.00.23
00.00.24
00.00.25
00.00.26
00.00.27
00.00.28

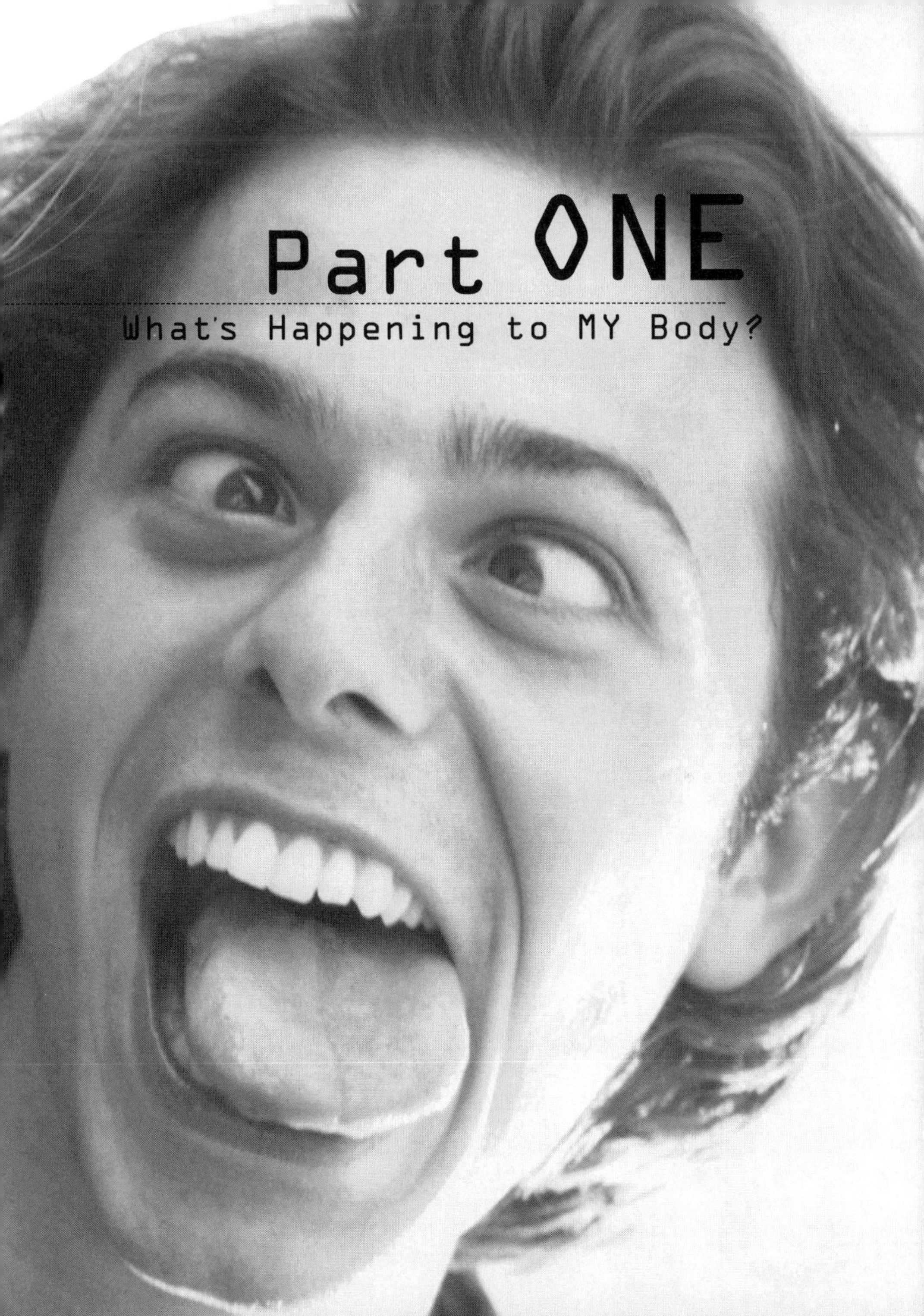

Part ONE

What's Happening to MY Body?

I love low-budget science fiction movies.

In *The Attack of the Killer Tomatoes,* mutant beef-steaks terrorize a major city—until National Guard soldiers ketchup with them. *Creeping Terror* features rugged drama as a killer carpet floors Lake Tahoe High School. And who can forget *I Was a Teenage Wolfman, Santa Claus Conquers the Martians,* and *The Terror of Tiny Town* (an all-

CHAPTER

1 When Will Puberty Start?

midget western)? Hey, I'm not making these up. Check the late-night listings in your *TV Guide.*

Japanese films—the lowest of the low-budget bombs—include such classics as *Godzilla vs. the Smog Monster, Godzilla vs. King Kong, Godzilla vs.* (fill in the blank with any radioactive moth, slug, tomato worm, or rickshaw driver).

Each of these movies stars a quite normal person, plant, or animal. Until ... an **alien** from outer space or fallout from a nuclear power plant turns him, her, or it into a hideous creature with uncontrollable powers. The highlight of the film, of course, is the slow-motion close-up of horrible mutation.

As the victim peers into the mirror, he realizes that something strange is happening. He begins to outgrow his clothes. Hair begins to sprout all over his body. His once-clear complexion breaks out with raw, red bumps. Then, with a bloodcurdling cry, he realizes that incredible powers have taken over his mind and body!

Wait a minute! That's not a movie—it's me at 13!

What on earth is happening inside my body?

Yep, physical, mental, emotional, social, and even spiritual "mutations" begin to transform you into a completely different person during this time of adolescence.

Suddenly, you discover your jeans are too short. Hair begins to grow under your arms and between your legs. Pimples begin to erupt all over your face. The simple, pat answers that you've learned since birth just don't seem to make sense anymore. Suddenly, Mom and Dad don't understand you. And with all these physical, mental, and emotional changes, you notice a big difference in how you view the opposite sex.

Why can't we just be born the way we turn out?

It would be nice if we could just be born this way and skip the angst of adolescence altogether—but our sexual organs don't begin working until we are physically ready to have children. And that's a good idea!

The name for this change from childhood to adulthood is *puberty*, which comes from the Latin word for adult. Puberty begins when your brain tells the pituitary gland, "It's time for a transformation!" This tiny gland, about the size of a small bean, then releases hormones into your bloodstream.

What is causing all these changes?

The word *hormone* comes from the Greek word for *excite*. (Now there's an accurate word!) During puberty, more than 100 "exciters" race through our bodies, controlling temperature, hunger, thirst, bone growth, and level of blood sugar.

But scientists are finding that strictly "male" or "female" hormones don't exist. Both guys and *girls* produce androgen (once thought only male) and estrogen (once thought only female). These chemicals stimulate the growth of hair and cause your sexual organs to mature.

Why am I not changing when all my friends already have changed?

Androgen and estrogen act at different times in different teens. So there are no normal ages for these changes—only what your hormone timetable says is right for you. Because of this, throughout the next three chapters, we'll talk about average ages—but "average" is not the same as "normal." For instance, let's say only two human beings inhabited the earth. One started puberty at 10 years of age and the other at 14. The *average* age of puberty would be 12, but neither of these two people would be "average"!

I hope that's comforting for the many teens who wrote to me and asked: Why did I start so soon? Why am I not changing as fast as everyone else? Why am I still so short? Why am I so much taller than everyone in my class? Why am I heavier than everyone else my age? Why am I skinnier than everyone else in the class?

The following chart shows the *average* ages at which these changes begin. Some of us may mature much earlier and some much later. So don't be worried if you're not "on schedule" with others your age—it's being on schedule

CHANGES	Female	MALE
Increase in growth	10—11	12—13
Hair between legs	10—11	11—12
Breast development	10—11	
Growth of scrotum and testicles		11—12
Menstruation	11—14	
Growth of penis		12—13
"Wet dreams" begin		12—13
Underarm hair	12—13	13—15
Development of sweat glands	12—13	13—15
Growth of voice box		13—14
Deepening of voice		14—15
Hair on upper lip		15
Facial and/or body hair		16—17
Pimples possible	14	16—17
Adult height reached	16—17	18—25

with yourself that really matters! And there's no such thing as a "late bloomer"—you'll "bloom" when your body's ready. Don't worry about it; sooner or later everything will even out.

Why are my feet and legs growing, but the rest of me isn't? When will my muscles start to get bigger?

We'll talk about specific changes for girls in the next chapter and for guys in the chapter after that. For now, let's look at some of the general changes everyone goes through.

General Changes

A lot of things happen during puberty. Young teens can gain from 25 to 30 pounds and grow four to six inches in one year. During this time, the heart doubles in size. Unfortunately, all parts of our bodies don't grow at the same rate. Head, hands, and feet reach adult size before the rest of the body. And legs grow faster than the top part of the body.

All this growing (and the eating that goes with it) begins when hormones cause an increase in the amount of protein produced by cells. This speeds up tissue development. That's why some teens can eat five hamburgers and still feel hungry. All that protein is going to fuel growing muscles.

I really feel weak sometimes. And, no, I don't smoke or take drugs. What makes me feel this way?

All this growing can be exhausting! "Growing pains" and feelings of fatigue are normal during this time. That's why 12- and 13-year-olds need more rest than they did at age 9 or 10. It's especially important to eat nutritional food during this time.

Are you really what you eat?!

If you eat your body weight at Pizza Hut's lunch buffet, you're not going to look like a Meat Lovers pizza. And if you simply nibble at the salad bar, you're not going to look like **Swamp Thing**. But your body does need healthy food to remain healthy.

Six major nutrients act as building blocks for a healthy body:

1. **Carbohydrates**–These nutrients come in the form of sugar and starch, which breaks down into sugar. These sugars provide fuel for our bodies. Bread, cereal, spaghetti, noodles, popcorn, and rice make up this category. Whole-grain breads and cereals contain fiber that keeps us regular and acts to prevent colorectal cancer. Fiber also may help reduce the "bad" cholesterol that clogs up our arteries.
2. **Protein**–Muscles, skin, hair, blood cells, and bones are mostly protein, which we get from milk, meat, eggs, cheese, nuts, beans, peas, and other protein-rich foods.

   Many researchers believe to live healthier, we must reduce the amount of red meat (which is thought to increase the bad cholesterol) and increase our intake of fish, chicken, and turkey. Instead of fried meat, eat boiled, broiled, or baked foods.

   The popular "Protein Power" diet, developed by Drs. Michael and Mary Eades, suggests that we need more protein in our diets and less carbohydrates to lower weight and cholesterol.[1] (Carbohydrates turn to sugars, which increase insulin production, which slows down metabolism and adds extra insulation.)
3. **Vitamins**–Vitamin A contributes to good vision. Vitamin B keeps our nerves, muscles, and skin in good shape. Vitamin C, along with vitamin E and beta carotene (the vegetable parent of vitamin A), is thought to protect us from those nasty "free radicals" that cause us to "rust." (We'll talk about free radicals in book two of this series, ***Is There Really Life after Death?)*** Vitamin D helps heal wounds and broken bones. Vitamin E keeps our skin smooth and may even boost our immune system. Vegetables, fruit, and milk are good sources of many vitamins.

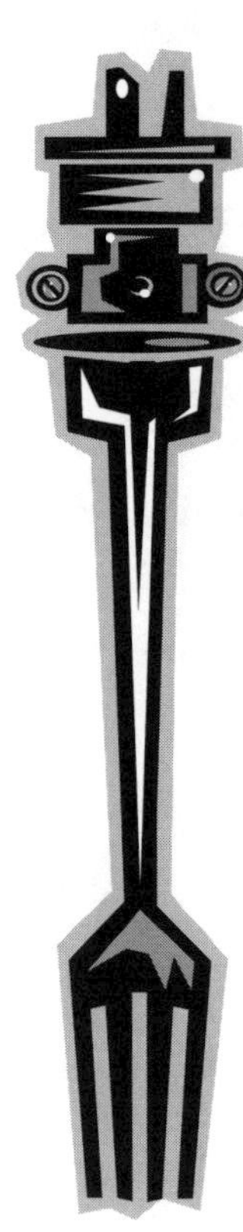

4. **Minerals**–Calcium and iron are two important nutrients. Calcium, found in milk, builds strong bones and teeth. Iron builds up our blood and reduces feelings of fatigue. Sources of iron include fish, chicken, turkey, lean red meat, and leafy green vegetables.
5. **Water**–Our bodies are made up of about 80 percent water, so it's a very important part of our diet. Doctors suggest you drink eight eight-ounce glasses of H_2O per day.
6. **Fat**–Despite the bad rap it's gotten recently, fat is an essential nutrient. It provides energy, transports vitamins throughout the body, keeps us warm in cold weather, and acts as a shock absorber for the internal organs. However, we don't need as much fat in our diet as most of us take in. (Sorry, Oreos are **not** considered a basic food group!)

We can get most of our nutrients by eating the following each day:

★ Two servings of meat, fish, or poultry

★ Three to four servings of dairy products (**Sorry**, Dairy Queen Blizzards don't count!)

★ One serving each of vegetable and fruit

★ Four servings of bread or cereal

Eating right and getting plenty of exercise usually will keep our bodies in good shape. If you still feel weak or are having a hard time with your weight, check with your school nurse or family doctor. They should be able to give you some helpful suggestions.

What is pubic hair for?

Why do you get hair under your arms?

Another very noticeable change—besides outgrowing your jeans every few months—is the growth of body hair. Pubic hair (the hair around your sexual organs) often appears straight at first, then curly. Hair under your arms comes later. These hairs really do have a purpose: They draw the moisture away from the pubic area and under the arms to avoid skin irritation and chafing.

Why do I now need to use deodorant?

Also during this time, **apocrine glands** begin to develop. They're found in the armpits, nipples, and genital areas. When we become nervous, angry, or sexually excited, these glands begin pumping out perspiration. Unfortunately, as many of us have discovered, when sweat combines with bacteria, it gives off a bad smell. Deodorant keeps underarms drier and freer of bacteria and so reduces odor.

Facial and body hair usually begin to grow on guys by the time they're ready for driver's training. Some believe that this hair protected our early ancestors from the weather. It does help keep body warmth in and cold air off the skin's surface. (I grew a beard recently and noticed that my face felt much warmer while I was shoveling snow.)

When will I start getting pimples?

The increase in hormones has one nasty side effect: **Acne!** Suddenly, your skin begins to make more oil than before. Normally, this oil lubricates your hair roots and keeps your skin soft—but when your body produces too much oil, it can plug up the hair follicles. This causes a painful red swelling (with which many of us are all too familiar). "Whiteheads" form when hair follicles become infected; "blackheads" are not really dirt, but dark skin pigment.

Guys seem to have worse cases of acne than girls—probably because males have more androgen and testosterone than females.

Acne is not caused by dirt, but by excess oils. Gentle face washing, especially when your face feels like an oil slick, helps remove the excess lubricant. But don't scrub off the first layer of skin with scratchy soaps or acne pads. This will cause your face to become more irritated and more likely to become infected.

Now the good news: Acne is not caused by eating chocolate, ice cream, or fried foods or by drinking cola or milk. (Researchers have discovered that those who are around fast-food grills have worse cases because of the oil in the air, not in their stomachs.)

How can I get rid of zits?

And there is more hope: You don't have to wait to "grow out of it." Here are some practical, simple things you can do now:

1. Avoid heavy makeup, greasy suntan oils, or any creams that add oil to your face.
2. Use acne medication that contains benzoyl peroxide. (Benzoyl peroxide can be irritating, though. Ask your family doctor or school nurse about the new medicines being introduced each year.)

Why is my hair so oily?

All this excess oil tends to make hair oilier during adolescence too. Regular shampooing usually takes care of the problem.

Why do I sometimes feel so happy one minute, then down the next?

Not only does puberty bring about physical changes, it also brings about emotional, mental, and spiritual changes. Researchers aren't sure if hormones actually cause mood swings or if all the physical and social changes that accompany adolescence cause teens to feel up one minute and down the next.

Any change—positive *or* negative—causes stress and insecurity. This is a normal part of puberty (which we'll talk more about in Part Two: What's Happening to My Mind and Emotions?). In my survey, many teens asked, "When do all these changes stop?" "How will I know when I'm done?" "How can you tell if you're really mature?"

It's fairly easy to tell when you're done changing physically. But how do you know when you've emotionally and mentally matured? That's a bit harder.

Many junior highers look to **18 as the "password" to maturity.** It's that pivotal birthday on which childhood and adulthood swing. If you're like most, you've been peeking through the door since you were 8.

At 18 you can vote, get married without your parents' permission, sign up for the military, own real estate, and go to adult bookstores and X-rated movies.

And at 18 you also can be tried and sentenced in court as an adult, which should remind you that with "mature" status comes adult responsibility. Once the legal umbilical cord is cut, you are responsible for your own actions. No more "Mom and Dad forgot to wake me up," "It's all my parents' fault," or "Mom and Dad will get me out of this mess."

Maturity is much more than just physical and legal adulthood. Following are some signs of true maturity:

1. Making choices based on what will be the best for you and others in the future rather than what feels good right now. (Just because it's legal doesn't always mean it's the responsible thing to do.)
2. Showing self-control without giving in to pressure from inner impulses or from outside forces.
3. Accepting the authority of others without rebelling against them or totally giving up your own views and values.
4. Accepting people and things the way they are, not pretending they are the way you want them to be. You can encourage people to be the best they can, but you also can accept that you can't force them to change.
5. Keeping promises and commitments no matter how difficult it may be.
6. Living in a Christlike manner.

It might be a good idea to photocopy this list and tape it to your bedroom wall. Throughout this book, we'll be talking about making mature choices in relationships, dating, sexuality, and many other issues teens face. This list will help you remember what mature responses are all about.

A big part of puberty for girls is the beginning of *menstruation.* Menstruation has many names—some of them not printable—but the most common is a *period.* (Menstruation comes from the Latin word *mensis,* which means *month.*)

During the years that a woman is capable of having children, her body goes through a 28-day menstrual

CHAPTER

What Is a Period? 2

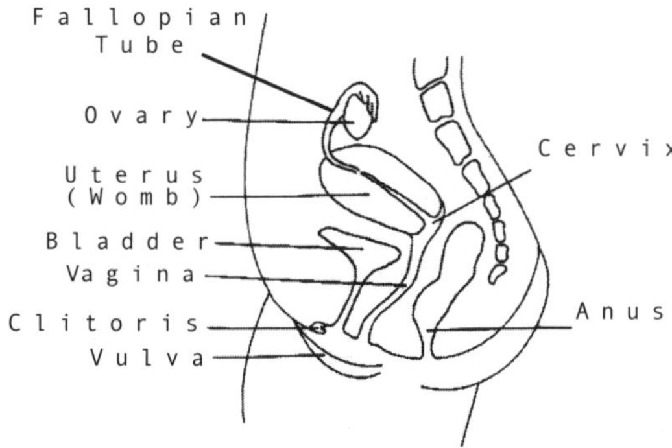

cycle. This prepares her body each month for possible pregnancy. (Remember when we talked about averages in chapter 1? Well, 28 days is the *average* length of a cycle. Some women's cycles are as long as 35 days.)

The ovaries, small flat glands in the lower part of a woman's body, make hormones and cause "unripe" eggs to mature. These eggs contain exactly half of the genetic material needed to create a baby.

Each month, one of the ovaries releases a mature egg into the fallopian tube. If a woman has intercourse (sex) with a man while the egg is in this tube, the egg and sperm may combine to produce new life. This is called *conception* or *fertilization. (It's also called "getting caught" if your unmarried!)*

The egg, whether fertilized or not, travels down the three- to six-inch-long fallopian tube and enters the uterus. The uterus, or womb, lies just above the bladder and serves as the "life-support system" for the growing baby. In anticipation of the arrival of a fertilized egg, hormones have caused the uterine lining, called **endometrium,** to become moist, soft, and thick with additional blood vessels. The egg "homes in" and nestles into the side of the uterine wall.

If the egg is fertilized, this new life continues to grow inside the uterus until birth. The baby receives food and oxygen from the mother's uterine wall through a cord called the *umbilical cord.*

If the egg is unfertilized, the extra tissue and blood supply are not needed and so are discarded. So for three to five days (again, an average), the blood and excess tissue move slowly through the *cervix* (the opening to the uterus), into the *vagina* (the tunnel to the outside of the body), and out of the body.

After the uterine wall returns to normal, the cycle begins again. So roughly every 28 days, the uterine wall thickens, and an egg is released. If the egg is not fertilized, the blood and egg flow out of the body.

The idea of blood passing from one's body may not be a pleasant thing to think about. It may be downright frightening, especially if those close to you talk about it as "the curse." But remember, this is a normal, natural part of being a woman.

One psalm writer describes this fearful and wonderful process:

> For You created my inmost being; You knit me together in my mother's womb. I praise You because I am fearfully and wonderfully made; Your works are wonderful, I know that full well. My frame was not hidden from You when I was made in the secret place. When I was woven together in the depths of the earth, Your eyes saw my unformed body. (Psalm 139:13-16a)

When will I start my period? I'm almost 14 and haven't yet.

Most girls begin this cycle between the ages of 11 and 13. African American girls tend to start a bit earlier. Girls who are very thin or athletic often start their periods as late as 17. If a girl is 16 and hasn't started her period yet, it's a good idea to see the family doctor just to be sure everything is okay.

Does it hurt when you have your period?

Periods often are irregular during the first year or two because ovulation tends to occur off schedule. Just remember that everyone is on her own unique timetable. The feelings that come with periods also are unique to each girl. Some have a dull to severe pain, called *cramps,* in the lower abdomen or back. **Cramps** usually are worse at the beginning of the period. Exercise and nonprescription pain medication can relieve much of the pain.

If the pain has begun within three years of the first period, it is probably caused by the hormonal changes. If the pain has begun after a few years of pain-free periods, a girl should see her family doctor. He or she can prescribe painkillers or drugs that will keep the hormone level in balance.

Some women have especially heavy or long periods. These are not uncommon and often occur in those who haven't established a regular cycle. During a period, girls should avoid strenuous activity and make sure they're getting plenty of vitamins and minerals to replace the iron that is being lost. If heavy bleeding lasts more than 24 hours, a doctor can prescribe medicine that will reduce the bleeding.

Why do I feel so down and irritable when I have my period?

Another side effect of menstruation can be emotional complications, often called *premenstrual syndrome* or **PMS**. About 40 percent of women experience mood swings (happy one minute, sad the next), slight depression, weight gain because of fluid buildup, and tenderness of the breasts. Only one out of 20 women in this group has severe problems. Doctors disagree about the cause of PMS. Some believe it's caused strictly by hormonal activity; others believe it's the result of emotional stress or problems.

In my survey, many girls wanted to know what kind of protection a girl should use while menstruating. That's a question best decided by the girl, her parent or guardian, and her doctor. Some of the most common forms of protection are sanitary pads, tampons, and a relatively new product called "Instead."

Pads are flat layers of fabric that absorb the blood and uterine tissue. These are worn outside the vaginal opening and often are attached to the undergarments by a strip of adhesive. Tampons are made of layers of fabric shaped into a narrow, round rod. They are inserted into the vaginal opening where they absorb the discharge. A strong string allows the tampon to be pulled out of the vagina after use.

In 1996, a new product called "Instead" was marketed. The soft plastic "cup" is worn inside the vagina and captures menstrual flow rather than absorbing it like a tampon. The cup can be worn for up to 12 hours, but it is rather difficult to insert and remove, and it sometimes leaks.

I heard tampons can make you sick. Is that true?

Very few women develop Toxic Shock Syndrome (TSS), believed to be caused by a reaction to synthetic fibers in tampons. Symptoms include fever, diarrhea, vomiting, muscle aches, and a sunburn-like rash. It can be fatal in rare cases, so a girl should contact her doctor immediately if she experiences these symptoms.

The risk of contracting TSS can be easily reduced. Use tampons that are 100 percent organic, such as all cotton. Don't leave tampons in for more than eight hours (use pads while sleeping). And wash hands before inserting tampons.

Will I lose my virginity if I use tampons?

In some cultures, unmarried women wouldn't think of using tampons or products like "Instead" for fear of tearing the *hymen,* a thin layer of skin over the vaginal opening. An unbroken hymen is proof of virginity in these cultures. Since a virgin is someone who has not had sexual intercourse, tampons really have nothing to do with losing virginity. In fact, the hymen can be broken in activities other than intercourse, such as strenuous sports.

When will my breasts start growing?

Another preparation a woman's body makes for motherhood is the development of breasts. Breasts are made up of 15 to 20 milk-producing *mammary glands.* These glands feed into the same number of openings on the nipple. Mammary glands are surrounded by fat deposits, which determine breast size. Since the actual glands—not the fat—produce the milk, breast size has nothing to do with the amount of milk a mother can produce. This milk is only produced in the last stages of pregnancy.

Breasts begin to "*bud*" between the ages of 10 and 11. During this time, they may become tender or sore. This is completely normal; it is not a sign of cancer or any other disease, as many girls fear. Often one breast will begin to develop before the other. Many mature women have one breast that is larger than the other.

When will my breasts stop growing? People tease me because they're so big for my age.

The size of a woman's breasts is determined by her genes. Many women's breasts continue to grow until they are in their 30s. A woman's breasts generally become somewhat larger during the premenstrual stage and quite a bit larger during pregnancy. But the size of a woman's breasts has nothing to do with womanhood or sexual fulfillment. Unfortunately television, plastic surgeons, guys in the locker room, and magazines such as *Playboy* have made a big issue over breast size. It's up to a young woman to choose how she will react to all the talk about breast size. ("Oh, just grow up, guys!" is a good response!)

According to one researcher, junior high boys think about sex every 30 seconds. I think that's a bit exaggerated—but only a bit! Guys do think about sex a lot more than girls—and for a good reason: That's the way they're made!

Inside the *scrotum* (the bag of skin that hangs

CHAPTER

Why Are Guys Always Thinking about Sex? 3

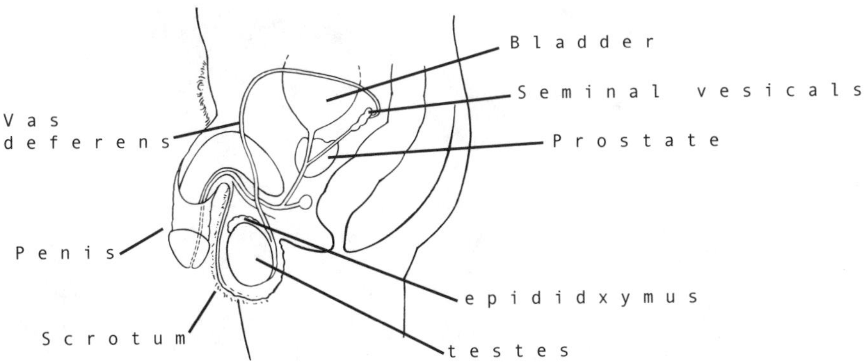

behind the penis) are two egg-shaped glands about one and a half inches in diameter called *testicles* or *testes*. One of the testicles often hangs lower than the other.

At about 13 years of age, these efficient factories begin to pump out *testosterone* (a hormone that creates sex drive in both men *and* women). They also manufacture up to 400 million sperm cells each day. Each sperm cell contains one half of the genetic material needed to create a baby.

This huge inventory of sperm is stored outside the testes in a maze of tubing called the *epididymis.* Testes are outside the main body because sperm don't grow well at normal body temperature. The temperature inside the scrotum is

about three to four degrees cooler than the rest of the body. During cold weather the scrotum shrinks, pulling the testes closer to the body and warmer temperatures. In hot weather or warm bath water, the scrotum becomes limp to move the testes away from the warm body.

After the sperm mature, they are transported through another set of tubes called the *vas deferens* into the lower body. In the *seminal vesicles*, sperm cells are mixed with a thick, milky fluid called *seminal fluid*, then stored. Once the epididymis and seminal vesicles are filled with sperm and seminal fluid, the physical pressure creates intense sexual drive in the male. Unfortunately, the sperm assembly line doesn't slow down once these "warehouses" are filled to capacity. All this seminal fluid needs to be shipped out!

Why do guys think about sex more than girls?

So, girls, understand that guys are preoccupied with sex for some very real *physical* reasons. However, girls, don't let a guy scare you into having sex with him for fear he's going to explode if he doesn't make love with you. Our Creator has equipped guys with a built-in "inventory reduction plan."

What causes an erection?

During the night, the bladder (the storage tank for urine) becomes full and presses against the seminal vesicles. When these sperm storage tanks are full, this pressure causes the penis to become hard and much larger. This change in the size of the penis is called an *erection*. During an erection, blood fills three "hydraulic cylinders" that run lengthwise inside the penis. The pressure causes the penis to become hard and nearly double in size. The seminal fluid is *ejaculated* (or forced) out of the body through the penis. Just before an ejaculation, a special "valve" shuts off the bladder so only sperm and seminal fluid pass out of the penis.

What are "wet dreams" and what causes them?

These involuntary ejaculations are called *wet dreams* (or *nocturnal emissions*) and are very normal. They're nothing for a guy to feel guilty or embarrassed about. (And Mom will not be shocked when she discovers the evidence while changing the sheets. She's aware that this is a normal part of her son's development.)

About one guy in 20 doesn't have wet dreams. This, too, is perfectly normal. There is nothing wrong sexually with a guy who doesn't have them.

Often guys resort to self-stimulation (or *masturbation*) to release sexual pressure. (We'll talk more about this in chapter 17.) At other times, erections are caused by sexual thoughts or tight clothing. And sometimes—believe it or not—they happen for no apparent reason at all.

What's circumcision? Why are some guys circumcised and some aren't?

When a boy is born, the end of his penis is surrounded by a flap of skin called the *foreskin.* Many doctors believe that circumcision—cutting off this skin—keeps the "head" of the penis free from bacteria that might collect under the foreskin. The American Academy of Pediatrics, however, believes that circumcision is not medically necessary. The U.S. Department of Health and Human Services reports that around 62 percent of newborn boys currently have this procedure.

For Jews and Muslims, circumcision also has religious meaning. The apostle Paul, however, declares it no longer has significance for Christians (see Galatians 5:6). For many parents, it's simply a decision based on tradition. So whether or not one is circumcised has little medical significance, and for Christians it has no effect on their relationship with God.

One boys' locker room "sport" is comparing penis size. But neither penis size nor circumcision affects the sexual pleasure of the husband or wife. (In fact, some studies have shown that shorter penises are more pleasurable to wives because a woman's most sensitive area is just inside the opening of the vagina.)

So just as girls should not be concerned with breast size, likewise no biological or medical reason exists for boys to be concerned about the size of their sexual organs.

Why do guys' voices change? Why does a guy's voice squeak when he's talking to a girl?

One of the last changes in male adolescence is the enlargement of the *larynx* (or *voice box*). This growth begins between the ages of 13 and 14. The noticeable drop in pitch—*nearly one whole octave*—usually occurs between 16 and 17. Embarrassing squeaks and changes in pitch are caused by this growth and sometimes by stress. But this, too, will pass!

As you finish reading these chapters, here's one note to remember: I've spoken of average ages in these three chapters. The only "normal" age for experiencing the changes we've covered is what is normal for your unique body! (You may want to underline that and put a star in the margin.)

Part TWO

What's Happening to My Mind and Emotions?

I'm really confused about who I am. When I'm with one group of friends, I act one way, and when I'm with another group, I act a whole other way.

CHAPTER

4 Who Am I?

Kevin was still sitting on the bench after everyone had left the youth camp assembly hall.

"Is there something I can help you with?" I tried to ask casually.

Kevin had impressed me as a guy who had it all. He was good-looking, and everything he wore sported a designer label. Plus, a parade of girls constantly followed Kevin around the campground.

"I don't know," he finally said. "I was just thinking about what you said about identity. Sometimes I just don't know who in the world I am."

Kevin, an eighth grader, is not alone in those feelings. Erik Erickson, a famous psychologist,

researched the different stages of development. He said that during adolescence, teens struggle with identity vs. confusion. (Who am I? What am I? Where am I going?)

In young adulthood, he suggests, the conflict involves intimacy vs. isolation. (Will I find someone to love? Can I really be honest and open with another person? Can I really know another person?)

In my work with teens and while speaking at youth camps, I've observed four major identity crises: self-identity, social identity, sexual identity, and spiritual identity. Let's look at each of these crises and discuss what they mean to you.

Self-identity

Do you ever look in the mirror and wonder who is staring back? Sure, your student ID card lists your name. But beyond some letters typed on paper, *who are you?* Are you your parents' son or daughter? Are you who your friends are? Or are you your own person?

The answer to this multiple-choice question is … yes.

We all think we are what we think other people think we are. (You may want to run an instant replay on that last sentence!) For example, if I think my parents think I'm a smart kid, I probably will think of myself as a smart kid. And I'll act like a smart kid. If I think my coach thinks I'm the greatest athlete since Michael Jordan, I'll think of myself as a great ball player. If I think my friends think I'm the next Robin Williams, I'll think of myself as a fun person. And chances are really good that I'll *be* a fun person.

During childhood, our thought patterns are shaped by our parents and other significant adults (such as relatives, teachers, and clergy). During adolescence, the power of influence shifts to other teens.

I noticed this in our daughter, Faith, when she entered junior high. Before we got out of the minivan at the mall, she always would plead with us, "Don't act like you know me." And when we watched her cheer at games, she wanted us to sit on the visitors' side of the gym. While living in Marion, Indiana, I used to speak several times a year at her school's assemblies. When we moved to a new school district where she was "Faith," and not "Mr. Watkins' daughter," she was thrilled.

This trend of moving from parents to peers as the most important people in our lives is a normal part of adolescence. (Sadly, it can create some real tension in the home. We'll talk about that in chapter 9.)

Right now, though, let's take a look at an important task of adolescence: discovering who we really are—apart from what our parents or friends think. Try using the following list of questions to focus in on your real identity. (And contrary to the rule about school books, you can write in this book!)

What's important to me?

____

____

____

What are my values and beliefs?

____

____

____

What am I good at?

____

____

____

What are my dreams for the future?

____

____

____

Where do I fit in this world?

____

____

____

Now, once you figure out who you are, it's time to consider another question: Do you really like what you are? I believe that's one of the toughest questions of all, the question of self-image.

Self-image, or self-identity, is how you feel about yourself. One of the most important things you can do is develop a healthy self-image, one where you see yourself realistically, recognize the good and the not-so-good, and accept yourself for who you are, for who God made you to be.

Unfortunately, self-identity also can be shaped, for better or for worse, by the messages you receive from others. If you think your parents think you're a stupid idiot, you'll think of yourself as a stupid idiot. And because stupid idiots don't do well in school, you won't bother to try.

Self-image can affect how you perform in every area of your life, from gym class ("I'm just a benchwarmer"), to the cafeteria ("Everybody thinks I'm stuck-up, so I'll just eat by myself"), to everywhere else.

I discovered that Kevin, the young man from the beginning of this chapter, suffered from a poor self-image. "I just feel so inferior sometimes," he admitted.

Inferior? I thought. *Let's talk inferior! People used to joke I was so skinny that when I was born the doctor tied me in a knot and spanked my umbilical cord. Inferior? I had braces and acne all through high school—***I looked like a pepperoni pizza with a zipper ...**

Kevin's voice brought me back to reality. "I look around at the kids here, and all I see is how much better they are than me. They're better looking, they play sports better ... just everything."

Comparison is often the first step to a poor self-image. We always can find people who look, talk, act, or think better than we do. Let's face it, very few of us could get our picture on the cover of *Seventeen*. Few of us use the bright, witty dialogue we hear on TV or in the movies (after all, they have script writers and rehearsals!). And it's a safe bet that never once have we or any of our friends saved the entire free world from destruction. (We probably haven't even held off five Ninja warriors with a broom handle!)

Unfortunately, well-meaning parents sometimes let us know that an older sister was better in math, that an older brother made varsity his sophomore year, or that a little sister keeps her room neater. School also becomes a battleground for self-image. Most teens get shot down by comparison: grades; clothes; picking teams; tryouts for band, cheerleading, or sports; and so on. All of these are based on comparison.

Copying is the next step to a poor self-identity. We find ourselves thinking, *If only I could be like them, I'd have it made! I'd be popular. I'd get invited to parties. I'd have a boyfriend or girlfriend.*

Copying plays an especially big part in fashion. An "unpopular" teen can wear the latest fashion craze from Europe, but until one of the "popular" teens wears it, the style won't catch on. I'm convinced that if the most popular girl in a school came dressed in a black trash bag, within a week every girl would show up in a black trash bag. (Okay, maybe I'm exaggerating just a little—but only a little!)

Unfortunately, simply copying the clothing, talk, or actions of others rarely leads to belonging or feeling good about ourselves. So ...

Criticism comes along. If we *can't* be like them, then we don't *want* to be like them: "Who wants to be in their little clique? They're a bunch of stuck-ups anyway." And off we go, tearing other people down to make ourselves feel better ... which never really works. Instead, we just end up full of dislike for others and for ourselves.

There is one way to avoid getting caught in this cycle: Discover the "real you" and be true to who that is. (We'll talk more about that in the next chapter.)

Social Identity

The second identity crisis you'll probably face is your social identity. No matter who you are, you're bound to be around other people. In fact, you're probably starting to realize that you actually *need* other people.

To understand your social identity, ask yourself these questions:

How do I fit into my family?

____

____

____

Where do I belong at school?

____

____

____

What do I contribute at church?

____

____

____

What are the groups or organizations I am involved in?

____

____

How come boys my age aren't interested in girls? I'm 12 years old.

During our teen years, we experience a trend in the social world: moving from same-sex friendships to opposite-sex relationships. This is accomplished in four steps:

1. In elementary school, girls and boys form their own same-sex groups. Because girls are "yuck" to boys, and boys are "gross" to girls, there's little interaction.
2. During junior high, guy-only cliques and girl-only cliques still exist, but now the distance between their turfs is shorter. The two groups begin to take an interest in each other. They voice this by teasing each other—an early junior higher's highest expression of affection.
3. Some of the girls and guys from the cliques eventually start talking and eating lunch together. Sexual segregation at school becomes less and less visible. A clique still does everything together as a group, but the membership of the clique now includes both girls and guys.
4. Finally, the guys and girls in the "gang" begin to pair off, forming two-person cliques. These cliques eventually become "couples."

Sexual Identity

Before children are 10 years old, they look pretty much the same from the waist up and the thighs down: two arms, two legs, one neck, and one head. Then puberty strikes. Suddenly, you move from being a generic person to being a "male" or "female." (Review the physical changes we covered in the last few chapters.) These changes in your body affect your sexual identity—who you are as a "male" or "female." We'll talk more about the mental, social, and spiritual dimensions of sexuality in later chapters.

Spiritual Identity

Not only do our bodies change dramatically, so do our minds and souls.

The movie ***The Wizard of Oz*** starts out in black and white, but after Dorothy lands in Oz, she opens the door to a brand-new world of living color. Almost as dramatically, in junior high brains shift from black-and-white thinking to a full spectrum of color. Before junior high, you most often saw only one obvious solution to a problem; now you can see many possible answers to problems.

This is a part of adolescence that probably drives your parents crazy. They used to give you an answer, and you accepted it as the only answer. Now you see several ways of looking at situations—not just Mom and Dad's way. In the teen years, our minds create theories and work them through. Children aren't mentally able to do that. (So be patient with your parents. All these changes are hard on them too!)

We also grow in our ideas of what's right and wrong. Lawrence Kohlberg, an expert in moral development, believes we go through six stages. I've listed those stages below, with my own phrases that I think fit them best.

1. "If it feels good, do it."

   This is the morality of small children: "If I let Aunt Mildred kiss me when she visits, she'll give me a present." "If I get slapped for chewing on power cords, I won't chew on power cords." A child has no sense that kissing Aunt Mildred or biting into 110 volts is right or wrong. One simply creates good feelings and the other doesn't.

   Unfortunately, some teens and adults still are in this stage of morality. Some will attend church merely because the music, pageantry, or ritual makes them feel good—even though they don't profess faith in God. True morality and true relationships go far beyond mere feelings.

2. **"You scratch my back, and I'll scratch yours."**

In this stage, we do only those things for others that we want them to do for us. There is no thought of loyalty, gratitude, or justice. It's simply "I'll meet your needs if you meet mine." There are still quite a few of these types in junior high.

Unfortunately, the church sometimes preaches this kind of morality: "If you obey God, He will bless you." "Give to the church, and God will give you health and wealth." This, too, is a stunted and incomplete view of morality.

3. **"If you'll like me, I'll do it."**

Good behavior pleases others and is rewarded. The question a person in this stage asks is not whether the action is moral or immoral, but whether people will approve of it.

Using this morality, street gangs enforce strict codes of conduct. Obviously, I'm not suggesting that drive-by shootings and drug dealing are moral. But because the members who do these things get a sense of belonging from fellow gang members, they *believe* these behaviors are "the right thing to do."

Unfortunately, some churches follow this line of moral thinking: "If you will just obey our list of dos and don'ts, we'll accept you." Members may have no personal relationship with God, but they are viewed as "saints" because they conform to the church's rules.

4–5. **"Because them's the rules!"**

While crawling around under the dining room table as a third grader, I discovered a mysterious tag stapled to the bottom of each chair: "Warning! Do not remove this tag under penalty of law."

I scrambled out from under the table, my little heart pounding with fear. I had no idea why the warning was there; I *just* knew I had to obey or I'd be eating off a long table in the state prison from then on. (I later discovered the warnings were for sneaky storekeepers who might switch labels that listed the chairs' materials.)

In this stage of morality, "doing one's duty," "respecting authority," and "keeping the peace" are right only "because them's the rules."

As a parent, I vowed I'd never tell Faith and Paul, "Because I'm the dad and I said so" when they asked, "Why do we have to ________?" Sometimes I've been successful in explaining that following the rules is not an end in itself but that there are practical reasons for following the rules and very real consequences for ignoring them. Other times, I haven't been so successful. But I try hard to help my kids in this area because I've seen the consequences of not understanding the reason behind the rules.

When my wife and I worked with university students, we counseled a lot of teens who had grown up with a "rules" mentality but who hadn't been taught the *why* behind the rules. So as soon as they arrived on campus, they broke every rule their parents and church had taught them. That's when they discovered the often painful physical, emotional, or social consequences of their actions.

Out of those counseling experiences, I realized there was a need to help teens think through rights and wrongs for themselves. (We'll talk more about that in book three of this series, *Are There Really Ghosts?*)

Rules, in and of themselves, don't keep us from wrong choices. The apostle Paul realized that. In Romans 7:14–17 he wrote: "The law is good, then, and the trouble is not there but with *me*, ... I don't understand myself at all, for I really want to do what is right, but I can't. I do what I don't want to—what I hate. I know perfectly well that what I am doing is wrong, and my bad conscience proves that I agree with these laws I am breaking. But I can't help myself" (TLB, emphasis added).

6. "Love is the reason."[2]

   In this level of morality, a person doesn't disobey rules but obeys them for the right reasons!

   At this level, we do what is right not because it feels good, or because we'll get something for doing it, or because people will like us for it, or because the rule book says we have to. We do it because it's the right, loving thing to do. Paul sums up this morality by writing, "Love does no harm to its neighbor. Therefore love is the fulfillment of the law" (Romans 13:10).

Growing beyond the first stages of morality is one of the struggles teens deal with. We begin to question a morality that says "conform" and "just follow the rules." This is a normal part of mental and **spiritual growth**. Sometimes parents view this as **rebellion**. And, unfortunately, sometimes they heap on more rules in response. Also the church often doesn't allow teens to ask sincere questions.

These momentous shifts create inner emotional **stress** for adolescents. Sometimes it may feel just as painful as those Japanese movie mutations seem to be. Instead of trying to calm ourselves down by telling ourselves, "It's only a movie, it's only a movie," we can assure ourselves, "It's only a stage, it's only a stage."

These changes also create social stress between you and your parents, teachers, and other authorities. Your natural reaction may be to rebel or just to stay in your room until you're **21**. What you need to do is talk honestly—yet respectfully and calmly—to those around you about these changes. Share with them what you're feeling and the emotions and thoughts that war within you. You may be surprised to learn they've probably felt the same way.

It may be helpful for you and your parents to read through this book together. There's even a section in the back to help your parents talk with you about the things that really matter right now. It's my hope that both teens and adults will realize that these identity struggles are a normal and healthy part of adolescence.

At least that's what I tried to share with Kevin, the eighth grader I mentioned at the beginning of this chapter. Finally, he stood and straightened his shoulders.

"Thanks for listening, Jim," he said. "I'm just glad to know that what I'm going through is normal. Maybe I can even help somebody else's identity this week."

"I think there's a good chance of that, Kevin," I said. And I meant it. His "groupies" were waiting for him at the assembly hall door.

It happens suddenly. Mom and Dad tuck you and your favorite stuffed animal into bed, reassure you there is no bogeyman, and turn off the light. But something happens during the night. Suddenly you're filled with strange and powerful emotions. Your mind isn't exactly dancing with "visions of sugarplums."

CHAPTER 5

What's Happening to My Emotions?

Part of the reason for this emotional upheaval is physical. (We talked about it earlier.) A good deal of your emotions, however, don't come from your hormones; they come from your head. Emotions—especially those tied in with sexual feelings—are a combination of what's genetically programmed into our glands and what we input into our brain.

I think the hardest part of growing up is the emotional part. Sometimes, it's really scary. Why me?

Picture a computer system. One of the first things you do every morning is boot up this ignorant piece of hardware. Each time you turn it on, it just sits there and stares at you with a blank phosphorescent look. And it will continue to be a stupid stack of microchips until you reeducate it.

You double click on the word processing (or Tetris) icon and, in a matter of seconds, everything your computer needs to know about the program is transferred from its hard drive to its RAM. This brief operation will determine its thinking process until you exit the program.

Now think of your emotions as a computer program. In the same way that you boot up a computer, each of us boots up our brain each morning. And the programming we give it will greatly affect our emotions and thinking until we turn in for the night. Believe me, a lot of data gets programmed into our central processing unit throughout the day.

Thinking about Yourself

What kind of data entry do you make about yourself? Is it positive or negative? Here are some excerpts from my survey. Do any of them sound familiar?

- ★ All of a sudden I've started hating the way I look, but I can't change it. What can I do?
- ★ I wish I didn't have the complexion of a pepperoni pizza.
- ★ I wish I could do something about this hair.
- ★ Why did I get stuck with the figure of a circuit board?
- ★ How come I'm the only one in class who doesn't understand algebra?
- ★ Why did my sister get all the talent?

Rather than booting our brains and bodies around our bedrooms, we need to **boot up some positive qualities about ourselves.** Admittedly, we may not have the best-looking "mainframe" or a gazillion gigabyte brain, but each of us has some great qualities.

Let's do some computing. In the space below, or on a sheet of paper, list three of your best qualities. (Come on, get a #2 pencil and actually do this!)

1. ____________________
2. ____________________
3. ____________________

Now, write down the sources of negative "self-talk." Is it fashion magazines that show only clear complexions and sexy figures? Is it music that emphasizes looks rather than inward qualities? Is it believing the negative comments of others at home or school? Write down those "bugs" in your inner circuits and think seriously about "deleting" them.

1. ____________________
2. ____________________
3. ____________________

Finally, write down three sources of positive "self-talk." List people or things that build you up.

1. ____________________
2. ____________________
3. ____________________

Keep this last list handy (you may want to photocopy it) so anytime your circuits start to overload with negatives, you can easily remind yourself that you have some really valuable qualities.

Thinking about Others

Not only do we think a lot about our own qualities, but we also keep analyzing data from others. Is it negative or positive? Again, our early-morning programming will determine how we treat others throughout the day.

Let's try to debug some of that input. Write down the sources of negative data about the people you come in contact with: parents, brothers and sisters, people at school and church. Again, think seriously about deleting them. (The input, not your little brother and sister!)

1. ______________________________
2. ______________________________
3. ______________________________

Now write down three sources of positive "self-talk" about these people.

1. ______________________________
2. ______________________________
3. ______________________________

Finally, list three positive qualities about the person you have the most negative feelings about.

1. ______________________________
2. ______________________________
3. ______________________________

Debugging negative emotions isn't easy. But it *is* possible. Paul wrote some good news nearly 2,000 years ago—and it's still as up-to-date as the latest psychology: "And the peace of God, which transcends all understanding, will guard your hearts and your minds in Christ Jesus" (Philippians 4:7).

Last year I didn't even notice girls, but now I can't think of anything else. A lot of times all I can think about is getting them in bed.

How can I control my thoughts?

The word translated as *guard* in the Philippians passage is really a military term in the Greek language Paul used to write his letter. It's like having a six-foot-seven, 250-pound military policeman stationed to guard and protect your heart (your inner self, will, desires, emotions) and your mind.

Psychologists call one part of this guard "sensory gating," which means your brain was created so it can only really concentrate on one thing at a time. For instance, you're watching the 50th rerun of Gilligan goofing up another rescue attempt. Right in the middle of the show, your mother asks you to take out the trash. You actually don't hear her because your "gate" is open only to the Skipper hitting Gilligan over the head with his hat. Suddenly your mom kicks the gate open by yelling in your ear, "Are you deaf? Take out the trash!"

We filter out much of the talk and actions around us because we're paying attention to something else. It might be possible to concentrate so hard on positive things that you "see no evil, hear no evil."

But it seems that someone or something is always sneaking through the gate: You're trying to get just the right temperature in the locker-room shower when the people on either side of you start in with "I know a dirtier joke than that!" Or someone shoves a *Penthouse* magazine under your nose in study hall. Or you're looking through the paper for the comics and can't help but notice the XXX movie ads.

That's exactly where the "guard" at the gate comes to the rescue! Our memory banks are divided into two sections—*short-term memory* and *long-term memory*. All information arriving from your five senses comes into the short-term section, remains for a short time, then is completely forgotten.

For example, have you ever looked up a number in the phone book and by the time you got to the phone you had forgotten the number? That's because short-term memory can be extremely short! How do you remember the number? If you're like me, you probably repeat it to yourself as you start to dial: "555-4321, 555-4321, 555-4321 ..." It's only by thinking about it over and over that it's stored in your long-term memory.

Paul gives a list of "passwords" for the types of input we should think about over and over:

> Finally, brothers, whatever is true, whatever is noble, whatever is right, whatever is pure, whatever is lovely, whatever is admirable—if anything is excellent or praiseworthy—think about such things. (Philippians 4:8)

No virus of negative emotions can get past those passwords! But certain magazines, books, friends, TV programs, or deliberate thoughts can program negative actions, attitudes, or feelings.

Write down three negative inputs that you could delete from your mind.

1. ______________________________
2. ______________________________
3. ______________________________

How can we deal with all the negative data that already has been stored in our brains? Psychologists have discovered that we forget old information when new information pushes it out.

Suppose you spent all night cramming for a math test. As you walk out of the house, you have all the answers. But one minute into the test, you discover you've lost all that information. **Somewhere between waiting for the bus and fourth period, it was deleted.** New information (who's carrying whose books, who's breaking up with whom, which girl or guy of your dreams decided to talk to you today) has forced out everything you knew about binomial equations.

In this same way, God's guard protects us by cramming our minds full of positive input.

Now, write down three sources that could provide positive input:

1. ______________________________
2. ______________________________
3. ______________________________

We'll talk more about deleting negative memories and dealing with negative emotions a bit later. For now, remember: garbage in, garbage out.

My name is Jimmy Watkins. I am 7 years old. My uncle's computer is fun to play with. I am going to help him write his book.

What is love?

Love makes you have puppies. Mom wouldn't let my dog out this week. She said, "Buffy is in love. We don't want any more puppies." I let her out when Mom wasn't looking. It made Buffy happy.

CHAPTER

6 How Can I Know if I'm Really in Love?

Love doesn't make people happy. That's what Billy Smith said. Billy Smith is in sixth grade. He knows everything. Billy Smith says, "Love makes you feel warm all over your body. It makes you feel light-headed. It makes your stomach go flip-flop."

I was in love last week. Mom took me to the doctor. I got a shot where I sit down. I didn't even get a lollipop.

My Sunday school teacher says that love is giving. I gave Betty Green the chicken pops. I gave Junior Jackson a black eye. But I think love is just giving good things.

My Sunday school teacher says that love is in the afternoon. And love is made out of chocolate pudding. That is what the commercial says. "Thanks for the love in my lunch box." Do you know what is in the lunch box? A can of chocolate pudding! Love also tickles your nose and makes you belch. The lady sings, "Canada Dry tastes like love." Ginger ale tickles my nose and makes me belch.

And the man and the lady on TV said that love can be put together. Last night I got out my Lego building blocks. I asked real nice. I said, "Please, can you help me make some love?" Daddy's head turned red. The veins on his neck stuck out. He said, "Never say that again!" I asked Billy Smith. Billy Smith is in sixth grade. He knows everything. He said that love is a four-letter word. You will have to eat soap if you say words with four letters!

My dad says I watch too much TV. He said, "Love is not in the afternoon. Love is not chocolate pudding. Love is liking somebody just the way they are."

I like Betty Green. She is in first grade. She is beautiful. She has a neat chipped front tooth. I ride my bicycle past her house without my hands. Today I even stood on my seat. She just yelled that I am mentally retired.

Mom and Dad love me just the way I am. Even when I got sick on the brand-new carpet. They loved me after I gave Buffy a haircut with the grass trimmer. Buffy still loves me too.

I know I am loved. That makes me feel good. It is like when I come in from outside when it is 300 degrees below zero. My nose is dripping down to the knees of my snow pants. My mom gives me a big cup of hot chocolate. It makes my insides feel warm. That is what love is.

I hope you love me, Uncle Jim. Buffy just wet on your notes.[3]

I have *got* to keep my office door locked! But in his 7-year-old way, Jimmy does point out some problems with this slippery word "love." Part of the problem is that we have one little word for emotions that are as complex as a computer manual!

Can somebody explain love? It's so confusing!

I say that **I love deep-dish pizza**. I love my brother. I love my best friend. I love my wife. But obviously, I don't love Lois the same way that I love pepperoni pizza. And I don't love my kids the same way that I love my wife.

Four Kinds of Love

The Greeks were smart enough to give the world Philosophy 101, gyro sandwiches, the Olympic games, and four—count'em, four—separate words for love.

Why is the term LOVE used so loosely?

Eros, a word that came from the Latin god of hormones, was used to refer to sensual or sexual love. I *eros* deep-dish pizza because it makes my taste buds feel good. In the same way, I *eros* the sensation of a sea breeze in my face, my ragged Indiana Wesleyan sweatshirt, hot tubs, and sexual pleasure with my wife.

Phileo and *storge* describe friendship love and feelings for one's family. I *storge* my mom and dad. I *storge* my kid brother. I *phileo* my old college roommate. I *phileo* all the people of the world. I *phileo* anybody who buys this book!

Agape love is a willful, deliberate, I-choose-to-love-you love. (The Latin word is *caritas* from which we get *charity*.) This love is not based on warm mushy feelings or even on a relationship. It is unconditional—just like the love Colts fans have for their football team, even during its usual losing season.

The apostle Paul provides us with a classic definition of *agape*, which is the kind of love God has for us.

> Love is patient, love is kind. It does not envy, it does not boast, it is not proud. It is not rude, it is not self-seeking, it is not easily angered, it keeps no record of wrongs. Love does not delight in evil but rejoices with the truth. It always protects, always trusts, always hopes, always perseveres. Love never fails.
>
> (1 Corinthians 13:4-8a)

With four words for love, things were less confusing in ancient Greece. When Marcus reached over in the backseat of the chariot and whispered, "I love you," in Daphne's ear, she knew exactly what he had on his mind. He was forced to choose one of the four words for what he was feeling.

Marcus could have said, "I *eros* you," which roughly translated would have meant, "Baby, you look hot in that robe. Why don't you take it off!"

He could have said, "I *phileo* you," which meant, "Let's be good friends." (Now there's a phrase we guys love to hear!) Or perhaps he could have said, "I *storge* you" or "I love you like a sister." (Girls love to hear that!)

Or he could have chosen, "I *agape* you," which meant, "I've thought this through and have decided that I am going to love you unconditionally no matter what comes our way."

So if someone whispers "I love you" in your ear, you may want to respond with, "Hold it right there. Let's define terms!"

Love Triangles

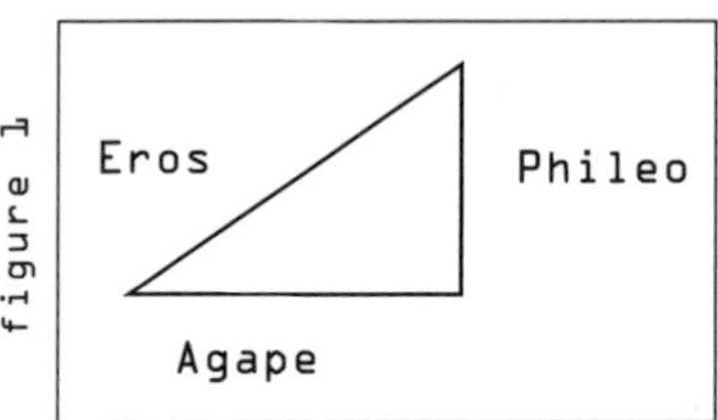

figure 1

During the dating period, many couples emphasize the *eros* side of the triangle (see figure 1). But Dr. Frederick Meeker of California State Polytechnic University believes the "half-life" of romantic love is about three months. (If, like me, you didn't do well in chemistry, that means if a romance has an intensity of "10," it will degenerate to a "5" in just 90 days. In six months, *eros* will have eroded to a 2.5 on the romance Richter scale.)[4]

That's why most relationships last about six months. Without adequate amounts of *phileo* and *agape*, the lopsided triangle comes crashing down. Love that lasts longer than dinner and a movie, then, is a healthy blend of *eros* (physical attraction), *phileo* (friendship), and *agape* (commitment). See figure 2.

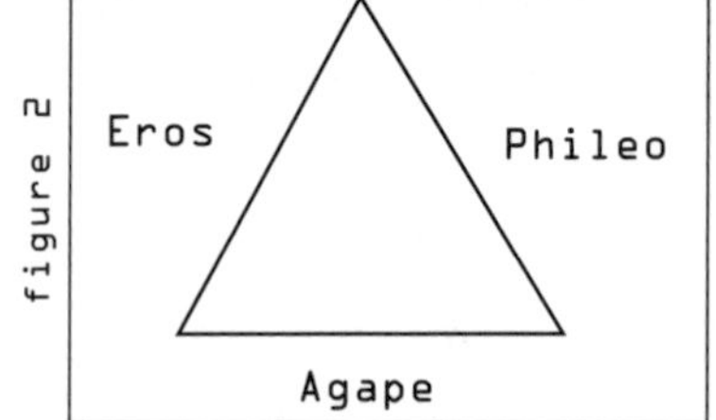

figure 2

Intersecting Love Triangles

The side from which we enter the "love triangle" also can have an effect on the stability of the relationship. We can, as Hollywood would want us to believe, approach love with our hormones (*eros*). But as we've said, *eros* usually has a diminishing dimension. In the rush of estrogen and testosterone, we're often blinded to the serious—and sometimes dangerous—flaws in our partner. (*Eros* love is not only blind, it's deaf and dumb![5]) That's why sometime around six months into a relationship, when the hormonal haze begins to clear, we start to wonder, "Why am I dating this person? What was I thinking?" When you enter a relationship from the *eros* side, very quickly you'll start looking for the "Exit" signs.

Another approach to the love triangle is with our hearts (*phileo*). Few people want to hear their potential partner say, "Let's just be friends," but this entrance does offer hope for a lasting relationship. Remember those human-interest news stories of couples who have been married for 75 years? (The ones who look like they've just been unearthed by an archaeologist?) The reporter asks the standard question, "What's the secret to a long marriage?" Inevitably, the two mumble through toothless gums, "We're each other's best friend."

Is it okay to love a lot of people?

Being "just friends" takes the pressure—and the masks—off a relationship. You see the person clearly, rationally, with all his or her strengths, weaknesses, good and bad hair days, emotional ups and downs, endearing and annoying habits, positive and negative interactions with other people in a variety of settings—the whole cafeteria line of life. And if you decide this is a person you'd like to spend a lot more time with, *eros* has a chance to develop along with the commitment of *agape.*

I approached Lois—like most hormone-driven males—from the *eros* side. (She was gorgeous!) She, however, had just broken up with a guy and only wanted to be friends. We dated a few times, but nothing erotic seemed to be happening, so I decided, "Well, if I can't have her as a girlfriend, I can at least enjoy having her as a friend."

So for months, we were just that. I thoroughly enjoyed heavy discussions with her over lunch in the college cafeteria about the Vietnam War, the oil embargo, whether the Beatles would get back together, life after death, whether *The*

Brady Bunch's Jan needed professional help, religion, and what type of people were marriage possibilities. She was smart, funny, loved to be with all kinds of people, and enjoyed most of the same things I enjoyed.

I'm really not sure what happened that fateful night in November of 1972. We were driving back from a concert with four other friends, and somewhere on I-294 west of Chicago, *eros* happened! I think it shocked us both. But by February 1973, we were engaged and thoroughly in *phileo, eros,* and *agape.*

Why is it that adults tell us we don't know a thing about love? There is a certain girl in my life who I want to be with all the time.

The final way to approach a relationship is with your head (*agape*), which would work fine for Mr. Spock of *Star Trek* fame or in countries where arranged marriages are still contracted. I'm not recommending this approach unless, of course, you're a Vulcan. But one arranged couple made a good point. "You Westerners bring the pot to a boil, get married, then take it off the stove. In Eastern cultures, we get married and put the pot on to boil. It starts slowly, but we keep it on the stove."

I know, I know: It sounds like a fortune cookie! But here's my point: Relationships entered into from the *eros* side face many more challenges for survival than those approached from the *phileo* front. But without the commitment of *agape* love, any relationship is in the express lane to Heartbreak City. (So if you want *agape* from your partner, and he or she is only interested in other forms of love, take the exit ramp!)

Scalene Love Triangles

That nice equilateral triangle of love begins to change shape with time. After observing thousands of couples, Dr. John Money believes romantic love begins to fade after two to three years. An old movie about marriage breakups is more optimistic with the title *The Seven Year Itch.* Actually, marriages that end in divorce have a median length (same number longer and shorter) of 6.8 years, but that doesn't make quite as catchy a title. So those who buy into the Hollywood illusion that love is strictly *eros* soon despair, then divorce.

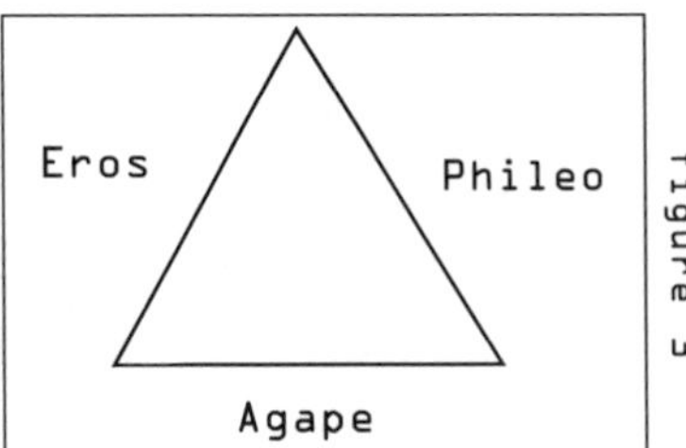

figure 3

Marriages, however, that are built on *phileo* and *agape* love can continue to mature and develop geometrically and physically—even if slightly out of shape (see figure 3).

Love that will last for a lifetime is not the "reel" love we see in movies (or hear on the radio), but it is the "real" kind found in a healthy blend of romance, friendship, and commitment.

So here's a "checklist," based on 1 Corinthians 13, for making sure love is real.

Patient

- ☐ I feel my partner is allowing time for the relationship to develop.
- ☐ I don't feel pressured to give more than I'm ready to give at this point.
- ☐ I feel he/she accepts my shortcomings and doesn't seem frustrated by them.
- ☐ He/she is willing to wait until marriage for intercourse.

Kind, not rude

- ☐ I don't feel embarrassed by my partner's behavior.
- ☐ My partner treats his/her parents/brothers/sisters with respect.

- [ ] He/she doesn't talk about people behind their backs.
- [ ] I would feel comfortable having this person as the parent of my children.

Does not envy, always trusts

- [ ] My partner doesn't get jealous when I want to spend time with my friends.
- [ ] There is mutual trust.
- [ ] Our relationship allows room to grow and develop. I don't feel smothered by my partner.
- [ ] We enjoy being apart at times.
- [ ] I trust his/her decision-making abilities.

Does not boast, is not proud

- [ ] I feel my partner is not just using our relationship to boost his/her ego or social standing.
- [ ] He/she doesn't brag to friends about our dates.
- [ ] My partner talks about others, rather than just himself/herself.
- [ ] He/she readily admits when he/she is wrong.

Is not self-seeking, always protects

- [ ] My partner uses words like *we*, *ours*, and *us* rather than *I*, *you*, *mine*, or *yours*.
- [ ] My partner doesn't ask me to do something that makes me feel uncomfortable.
- [ ] I'm convinced he/she has my well-being—physical, mental, emotional, social, and spiritual—in mind.
- [ ] My partner is unselfish in his/her actions toward his/her family and friends.

Is not easily angered, keeps no record of wrongs

- [ ] We can calmly discuss our differences.
- [ ] My partner allows me to be myself.
- [ ] My partner knows I have lots of faults but doesn't bring them up in an argument.
- [ ] When we're having a problem, I can always tell my partner what is bothering me.
- [ ] I feel completely safe with my partner.

Does not delight in evil, rejoices in good

- [ ] We can be completely honest with each other.
- [ ] My partner doesn't say, "I told you so!"
- [ ] My partner's conversations are pleasing to God.
- [ ] He/she doesn't gossip.

Always hopes

- [ ] My partner has a positive outlook on life.
- [ ] Our trust in each other is growing.
- [ ] This relationship is making each of us a better person.

Always perseveres

- [ ] Our relationship is steady, even though our emotions may have their ups and downs.
- [ ] My partner wants to be around me when I'm at my worst, as well as when I'm at my best.
- [ ] I think I could live with him/her for the rest of my life.

How do you make love last forever?

As you read the list above, you may have thought, *Who can love like that?* The Bible says

1. Love comes from God.

   Dear friends, let us love one another, for love comes from God. (1 John 4:7a)

   Many people think God is only interested in rules. But God is all about love. Jesus, God the Son, reminds us of the most important "rule":

   "'Love the Lord your God with all your heart and with all your soul and with all your mind.' This is the first and greatest commandment. And the second is like it: 'Love your neighbor as yourself.'" (Matthew 22:37–39)

   "Okay," we say. "That sounds good." But we seem powerless to love like that.

   Those who say, "I love God," and hate their brothers or sisters, are liars; for those who do not love a brother or sister whom they have seen, cannot love God whom they have not seen. The commandment we have from Him is this: those who love God must love their brothers and sisters also. (1 John 4:20–21 NRSV)

2. The power to love comes from God. Everyone who loves has been born of God and knows God. Whoever does not love does not know

God, because God is love. This is how God showed His love among us: He sent His one and only Son into the world that we might live through Him. This is love: not that we loved God, but that He loved us and sent His Son as an atoning sacrifice for our sins.

(1 John 4:7b-10)

Anything we have done that is not loving separates us from a loving God. We don't have to murder or commit armed robbery to "sin." Sin is simply breaking God's commandment to fully love Him and others.

If we claim to be without sin, we deceive ourselves and the truth is not in us. (1 John 1:8)

But God's only Son, Jesus Christ, died and rose again to atone for our unloving behavior (see 1 John 2:1–2). **Atone** means to make **at one**. When we confess our lack of love (sin) and believe that Christ has died and risen for our sin, we are forgiven and are "at one" with God and His love (see 1 John 1:9).

If anyone acknowledges that Jesus is the Son of God, God lives in him and he in God. (1 John 4:15)

3. The power to love unselfishly comes from God.

Love from God is not earned—it is a free gift—but it is *learned.*

No one has ever seen God; but if we love one another, God lives in us and His love is made complete in us. (1 John 4:12)

We get to know God and His love better through reading His love letter (the Bible), talking to Him (prayer), and being with those who also love Him (the church.) And the better we know God, the easier it is for us to obey His commandment to love Him and others.

This is love for God: to obey His commands. And His commands are not burdensome, for everyone born of God overcomes the world [of sin]. (1 John 5:3-4a)

If you'd like more information about strengthening your faith relationship with God, talk to your minister or Christian youth leader. Or you can write me in care of the publisher (the address is in the introduction to **The Why Files** on page 12) or e-mail me at whyfiles@jameswatkins.com.

Jennifer and Nathan sort of bumped into each other at a youth group roller-skating party. Actually, collided is a better word.

Nathan and his friends were leaving the snack shop just as Jennifer and her friends were entering. Suddenly the law of physics that states "two bodies

CHAPTER

7

How Do You Fall —and Stay—in Love?

cannot occupy the same space at the same time" was proven true.

Nathan scrambled to help Jennifer up. As their eyes met, it seemed that time stood still. The music faded. Their friends disappeared into the background. It was just the two of them in one of those magical, slow-motion encounters from "chick flicks."

"I'm really sorry ..." Nathan paused, waiting for her to give him her name.

"Jennifer," she said and smiled at him.

"Are you okay?" he asked.

"Yeah, I'm fine."

"I'm really not that bad a skater once I get off this

carpeting, Jennifer."

"Maybe you can show me how well you skate." Jennifer took Nathan's hand as the deejay announced, "The next skate will be for couples only. Couples only."

By the time the announcement came for the last skate of the evening, Jennifer and Nathan were sure they were in love.

Is there really such a thing as "love at first sight"?

Sigmund Freud, the Austrian psychoanalyst, was one of the first people to try to "scientifically" study this thing called love. He claimed that a person doesn't actually "fall" in love or discover "love at first sight." Instead, *Freud believed we grow into love and love grows in us*, beginning in infancy. Yep, infancy!

Other researchers believe we begin to fall in love even before we're born. Here's how they explain it:

> For nine months there was oneness between you and your mother. No "Mom" and "me," only the warm, dark oneness of the womb.
>
> Even before you were pushed, kicking and screaming, down that dark tunnel toward the bright light, you

still viewed the world outside the womb as a part of yourself. The hunger in your little tummy and the breasts that fulfilled that need were one. The need for comfort, protection, and a dry bottom were one with the warm, caring blurs that came running at 3:00 in the morning to meet those needs. Everything from the crib to the diaper wipes to your parents was viewed as part of your being. There was no "me" or "thee"—only warm, wonderful "we."

Then came a shocking discovery! There was something out there that was not "we." Your body, blanket, and dry diapers were not one. And, most frightening, the warm, loving blurs were not one with you at all. They were very independent beings known as Mommy and Daddy. The splintering of your private world was frightening.

Child development experts believe "the terrible twos" syndrome is our reaction to the discovery that we are not the masters of the universe. Our world has not only been splintered, but it's now out of our control!

During late childhood, we made one last-ditch effort to regain our sense of power. **We dreamed about superheroes.** Perhaps Wonder Woman or Superman could reassure us that mere mortals could have superpowers. But by the first day of junior high, most of us had come to the awful conclusion that human beings are pretty powerless and often very alone.

M. Scott Peck, the author who has taken *The Road Less Traveled,* speaks of these feelings of separation and loneliness as "ego barriers."[6] The barriers between babies and parents are mostly physical. As children develop, however, other barriers block their inbred desires. For instance, there comes a day when guys are no longer allowed to go with Mom into the women's rest room. Perhaps Dad stops roughhousing with his daughter because she has begun to "mature." The first day of day care or kindergarten brought another assault on the oneness of early childhood. ("Wait! Don't leave me here, Mom! Hey, I don't know these people! I've seen undercover investigations on TV about these places! Don't leave me!")

Ah, but once we meet that emotional "image" of our future spouse (and he or she actually says "yes" to dinner and a movie), these "ego barriers" begin to collapse. We begin to experience that wonderful feeling we call "falling in love."

Why do older people say that young people don't really fall in love?

Once again we sense the power we lost in infancy. There is nothing the two of us—Superman and Wonder Woman—can't do as long as we have each other. We will accomplish all our goals. We will defeat every foe. We will live happily ever after. (Yikes! My blood sugar level is rising just writing this!)

Why doesn't love last very long?

Unfortunately, these wonderful feelings don't last long. The "terrible twos" also occur in relationships. Gradually, we discover that our loved one is not merely an extension of our own ideas, dreams, and desires. This rude awakening usually occurs within just a few months, when the strong emotional feelings begin to fade.

When this occurs, the couple can choose either to find someone else to "feel" in love with or can go on from baby love to a deeper, more mature love. Many choose to look around, which is fine for the junior and senior high school years. This also explains why many divorces occur in the first two years of marriage. Too many couples never get beyond the "feeling in love" stage. They don't understand that this is only the early stage of lasting love. Instead, they move from one relationship to another, to another, to another.

How do you make love last?

For relationships to last, we need to understand the practical aspects of a solid relationship.

For instance, when I talk at youth camps about love, dating, and sex, there are always three kinds of campers: pranksters with shaving cream and water balloons, campers who attempt to create the world's tallest human pyramid, and couples out in the woods. The couples out in the woods could learn some important lessons from the pyramid builders.

Pyramid builders are always careful to pick the strongest (or at least the biggest) campers to create the foundation. They know that without a solid base, the whole structure will collapse. In a relationship, that base cannot be the fragile feelings of *eros*.

Common Values and Beliefs

A solid relationship needs common values and beliefs for a rock-solid foundation—or at least something more than both of you loving deep-dish pizza, the Pacers, or alternative music. Feeling a mystical attraction to a person may spark a relationship, but romantic feelings can't hold up a relationship for more than a few months.

Now, take out a #2 pencil and a fresh sheet of paper (or write in the book—go ahead, it's okay!). Answer these important questions:

1. How do you and your partner view the world? Do you believe people are basically good or typically self-serving heathens?

___

___

___

2. What's your philosophy of life? Does having a life philosophy even matter?

___

___

___

3. What are your religious convictions? Political persuasions?

___

___

___

4. How do you think about money, and how do you spend it?

___

___

___

Okay, okay, this is a little deep for the first couple of dates, but a relationship that is going to last needs to have a solid foundation of common values and beliefs.

Common Goals

Do the two of you have the same goals? These make up the second level of the interpersonal pyramid.

A relationship is going to teeter and collapse if your goal is to become a Peace Corps volunteer and your partner is planning to be a trader on Wall Street.

While in Portugal speaking at a conference, I saw a wonderful example of common goals while watching farmers plow with oxen. Each pair of oxen pulling the plow was tied together by the horns. Both animals were forced to look in the same direction in the yoke. Before we **"yoke up"** with a person, we'd better be sure we're headed in the same direction. If not, the strongest ox will determine the direction of the pair. If both are equally strong (and bullheaded), then both will end up with a pain in the neck and little progress toward their goals. Most of the time, however, the "team" breaks up.

Common Backgrounds

One of the advantages of being a 98-pound teen was that I always wound up on the top of human pyramids. Common backgrounds are the "lightweights" that top off the interpersonal pyramid, but without them the stability of the structure can be affected. I am not suggesting that we become racists or economic snobs, but each difference added to a pyramid does create additional challenges to maintain balance. So know the differences between you and your partner and be prepared for their effects.

For instance, Lois and I came from very different backgrounds: Lois came from a family of seven living on a dairy farm who never did any vacationing, and I came from a family of four living in the suburbs who had seen most of the lower 48 states by my senior year of high school.

I was horrified that Lois' family would sit around the dinner table and discuss the very cow you were eating for dinner. **"Bossy was a good producer until she got mastitis."** I did manage to learn the difference between a heifer and a Hereford, but there was constant tension. Lois' parents thought I was—and I quote— **"a silly city boy"** who didn't know how to "work by the sweat of his brow." (Hey, *you* try to write a book!)

Lois continues to be frustrated by my concept of a vacation. I've seen most everything from Cypress Gardens to Fisherman's Wharf, so vacation to me means staying home, closing the curtains, and letting the answering machine take calls. Lois, however, wants to drive halfway across the country and stop at every tourist attraction from Ralph's Reptile Refuge to those other rip-offs with the word *Wonder* in the name.

That's just the minor stuff. Growing up in a smaller family, I wanted two kids; Lois wanted three. I'm more liberal; she's more conservative. Her family puts the toilet paper on the holder so it feeds off the back bottom side; my family prefers top and front. On and on and on ...

Opposites may attract, but they soon *attack* without agreement on the most basic issues. But because Lois and I are in conformity with our core values, beliefs, and goals, the pyramid is still standing after more than 25 years. It occasionally teeters, but it's still upright.

Oh. Jennifer and Nathan? They discovered they had more in common than roller-skating and are still going steady.

Most of us have groaned *I could just die* when we've tripped that special person on couples skate, spilled our tray in the cafeteria, or had an acne attack before a big event. Wanting to escape an embarrassing situation is a common and normal feeling.

But many teens, when faced with breaking up, a bad

CHAPTER

Why Do I Feel like I Could Just Die? 8

report card, sexual abuse, pregnancy, or some other crisis, begin to consider getting rid of their problems permanently—by taking their lives. More than 5,000 young people between 15 and 24 kill themselves each year. That same number attempt suicide every day. In light of these sobering numbers, it's clear that both adults and teens need to take the stress teens face seriously.

As you encounter times of stress, here are some things to be aware of.

Down Times Are Normal

Every person, when faced with a disappointment, loss, or tragedy, goes through five stages in dealing with it.[7] One stage is *denial*: "This just isn't happening." "We'll get back together some way." "I just think my cycle is off. I'm not really pregnant." "I was just dreaming. It really didn't happen."

A popular TV show neatly resolved the final cliff-hanger episode by making the entire season just a bad dream. The final episode of a popular TV comedy that had run for eight years revealed that the entire series was simply a nightmare.

But in the real world, we usually wake up and realize our problems are not a dream; they can't be denied. That's when the second stage kicks in and denial often turns to *anger*—anger at others, anger at oneself, and, especially for believers, anger at God. "God, if You're so loving, why did You let this happen?" is a common and normal cry. Remember, God will not love any of us less for voicing anger and bitterness. It's a necessary—and even healthy—part of dealing with difficult situations. God knows and understands that.

The third stage of dealing with difficult situations is ***bargaining***: "God, if You'll let Jan and me get back together, I'll go to church more often. I'll even put more in the offering plate. And here's an offer You can't refuse: How about if I become a missionary? You name it, I'll do it!"

But God rarely responds to this version of Let's Make a Deal. It's not that He doesn't care about our hurts and disappointments. It's just that He knows the best thing He can do is go through life's difficulties with us, not *poof!* make all our problems go away.

Sometimes I get so depressed. Am I the only one who feels that way?

The fourth stage we face is *depression*. Even saints such as Moses, Elijah, and Jonah went through periods of extreme depression and, yes, suicidal thoughts!

(Check out Numbers 11:10–15; 1 Kings 19:1–5; and Jonah 4:9.)

A list of the symptoms of depression is included in the next chapter. (Also, in the second book in this series, *Is There Really Life after Death?* we spend much more time discussing grief and depression.) If you're experiencing any of these symptoms, don't worry. Be encouraged that this is probably a normal phase of dealing with a crisis or disappointment. As you work to deal with the emotions you're facing, also keep in mind that

Down Times Are Temporary

No matter how bad you may feel now, it's probably only temporary. Most times of depression last only a few hours or days. Very few last a month or more. Be encouraged that if you get some outside help, feelings of depression don't have to be permanent.

You will, without a doubt, have high days and low days in your life. But mostly there will be ordinary days.

You know, the ones were you just go through the motions of school, home, or church. They're not bad days, but they're nothing to write your e-mail "buddy list" about, either.

I seem to get depressed for no real reason. Why is that?

It's interesting that the kinds of days we experience often follow a pattern. People seldom have only low days or only high days or even only ordinary days. We experience them all, at varying times, for varying lengths of time. And they can be triggered by all kinds of things. A girl's monthly cycle, sickness, lack of sleep, high and low air pressure, seasons of the year, or even eating pepperoni pizza at midnight can affect our moods.

There are also certain times of the year when suicides happen more often. November seems to have the most suicides of any month. It looks depressing when the days are growing colder and darkness is increasing. Upcoming holidays often emphasize family problems or breakups (you won't be together or you won't be looking for a present for a special person this year).

There are low days on the school calendar too: the week before finals, term paper deadlines, the first or last day of classes (depending on if you love or hate school). February 14 can be a low day if you don't have a valentine or a date for the big school party.

Anniversaries of a loss or tragedy can bring the low days back each year, often in living color and stereo sound.

But there is hope!

Down Times Can Be Overcome

Believe it or not, the prophet Isaiah had some down times too. He wrote:

[God] gives strength to the weary and increases the power of the weak. Even youths grow tired and weary, and young men stumble and fall; but those who hope in the LORD will renew their strength. They will soar on wings like eagles; they will run and not grow weary, they will walk and not be faint. (Isaiah 40:29–31)

Down times (even occasional thoughts of despair) are normal ingredients in life. It may take some time to get over the feelings of hurt and disappointment, and that's tough because we live in an instant society. We're used to instant drinks, microwave popcorn, and fast food. Sometimes we think our emotional state should change in 30 seconds or less. Just add a little alcohol or drugs to taste, our friends may suggest. Even some churches offer instant recipes: Just pray about it and all your problems will instantly disappear. But none of these instant cures work.

It's true that the only one who can help us endure and overcome the bad times is God. He is powerful and able. But He isn't a vending machine or a magic wand that will just make it better. As I said before, He is there to go through our low times with us, not to make the low times disappear. He is the one who can lead us, through human as well as spiritual help, into the fifth stage: *acceptance.*

I feel so tired and worn out all the time. Is that just part of changing so fast now?

When we reach this stage, we start to discover some very helpful tools: physical rest, spiritual restoration, and professional resources.

Physical Rest

Amazing but true: The cure for depression may be as simple as getting caught up on sleep! Here's part of a letter from a teen named Brad:

Last year, I was really hopping to keep up. I had a full schedule of accelerated courses. I was in the choir, in the school play, had a paper route, was the youth group treasurer, and was trying to keep honor-roll grades.

About January, I was physically and emotionally wiped out. I couldn't care less about anything. I just sat there like a zombie. I got nothing. I gave nothing. I was getting depressed.

I finally told our youth sponsor about my schedule. She said I didn't need to go to a doctor or the minister. I just needed to go to bed.

Anyway, to make a long story short, I got out of several of those things and began to get more sleep each night. What a difference!

In a month's time, I bounced back and was full of joy that I hadn't felt for so long.

Spiritual Restoration

Sometimes what we call depression is actually the emptiness we feel when God is left out of our lives. If you skipped over the end of the last chapter, you'll want to read it to see how God wants to help in this area of your life. You may be amazed what a difference He will make!

Professional Resources

If you have had long-lasting feelings of depression or thoughts of suicide on a regular basis, you need to talk to a professional. Your first stop should be your family doctor. He or she can help you find out if there is a physical cause for your depression. Researchers have discovered that chemical imbalance in the brain frequently is the cause of clinical depression. Prescription drugs often easily correct the problem.

I heard that you have to be insane to commit suicide. Are you insane if you only think about it?

No, you don't have to be insane to commit suicide or even to think about it. Many "sane" people get depressed enough that they contemplate suicide. If you need emotional help, your pastor, youth director, or school counselor may be able to help you. If they can't help, they can refer you to others who can. Always remember, there is hope!

Remember, too, that down times are normal. Even occasional thoughts of ending it all are not unusual. Down times are temporary, and they can be overcome with the right help. You don't ever have to be overcome. Believe it!

I have a friend who really scares me. She keeps saying things like, "I wish I was dead." What can I do?

Even if you're not dealing with depression yourself, chances are good you have a friend who is struggling with this emotion. You may even have a friend who is talking about suicide as the "answer." If this happens, there are some important things you can say or do to help.

First, don't try to handle it on your own. You're not a professional. You need to talk to your youth leader, counselor, or pastor about ways to help your friend.

Second, follow this list of suggestions:

1. Know the signs. Your friend may be thinking about suicide if he or she is
    - ★ Going through mood swings.
    - ★ Showing signs of depression. These signs include lack of concentration; deep-rooted boredom; withdrawal; eating too much or too little; lack of energy; self-criticism; negative thinking; feelings of guilt, shame, fear, or helplessness; rebellion; over-confidence; lack of fear of injury or death.
    - ★ Having problems at school.
    - ★ Having problems communicating.
    - ★ Displaying any sudden change in behavior. A sudden improvement in attitude may mean he or she has made the decision to commit suicide and now feels a sense of relief or control.
    - ★ Increasing the use of alcohol or drugs.
    - ★ Giving away personal property.
    - ★ Displaying self-destructive behavior.
    - ★ Talking about suicide, particularly the specifics of how.
2. Know what to do if your friend talks about suicide.
    - ★ Always take talk about suicide seriously. Never say, "You're not really going to kill yourself" or "You don't have the guts to do that." Assume your friend means exactly what he or she is saying.
    - ★ Pray that God will help you stay calm and compassionate.
    - ★ Assure your friend of your concern and God's love for him or her, even if that person has disobeyed Him. Also, assure your friend that feelings of depression are natural and can be overcome with proper help. Try to convince him or her that suicide is a permanent "solution" for a temporary problem.
    - ★ Don't promise to keep secrets about suicidal talk or attempts if your

friend won't seek help on his or her own.

- ★ Offer to go with him or her to talk to a professional.

3. Know what to do if your friend makes specific plans to commit suicide.
   - ★ Tell your friend you are not going to leave him or her alone and you are calling for help, then do it! Call 911, the police, a suicide hotline, the mental health clinic, or your pastor or youth worker. Don't leave the person alone until professional help arrives.
   - ★ Again, don't try to handle the situation by yourself.

If, tragically, a friend of yours or someone you know does end his or her own life, it's easy to feel that you somehow let that person down or could have done more to keep him or her from committing suicide. Such feelings are normal but seldom true. Suicide is a desperate—often irrational—action by the person who commits it. (We'll talk more about suicide in the second book in this series, *Is There Really Life after Death?*)

Part THREE

What's Happening to My Social Life?

Why can't we be treated like young adults? Most people treat teens like brain-dead children. We're young adults, so why can't we be treated like we're worth something?

CHAPTER

9 Why Do My Parents Get on My Nerves?

I've developed a few theories after being a teen for seven years, working with young people for more than 20 years, and being a dad of two teenagers.

The Pimple Principle

The number of blemishes in the eighth-grade class is equal to or greater than the number of times parents will say:

- ★ "When I was your age, I walked 10 miles to school—through five feet of snow."
- ★ "I hope you have kids just like you someday."
- ★ "When I was your age, I had to be in bed at 9:00." (And, of course, "I was up at 4:00 in the morning milking 15 cows.")

- ★ "Your room is a disaster area!"
- ★ "Turn down that stereo!"

Curfew Corollaries

Corollary One: No matter how soundly they are sleeping, parents wake up one minute past your curfew.

Corollary Two: Curfews [no matter how late] are always one hour too early.

Murphy's Music Theorems

1. There is a 75 percent probability that parents will be listening to "Groovy Hits of the '60s" (or worse yet, *singing* groovy hits of the '60s) when a teen's friends come over.
2. The higher the ranking on the song charts, the lower the volume of that song parents can endure. (For centuries, parents worldwide have complained, "All that music sounds alike and I can't understand the lyrics.")
3. Parents actually enjoy "easy-listening" music. (Remember, today's alternative music is tomorrow's elevator music.)

The Asparagus Postulates

1. Parents didn't like green beans, lima beans, broccoli, or asparagus when they were teens. (Sublaw number one: Taste buds change at 21.)
2. Allowances (no matter how large) are always a dollar too small.
3. Your parents are the ones who end up being youth group sponsors or chaperones on overnight trips.
4. Parents never ask, "Have you done your homework?" when teens actually have done it.

The Freedom Formula

1. The amount of freedom given to a teen is in direct proportion to the amount of obedience exhibited by the teen toward the parent.
2. The amount of trust a parent places in a teen is in direct proportion to the amount of honesty exhibited by the teen.
3. The number of privileges given to a teen is in direct proportion to the amount of responsibility exhibited by the teen.

For the visual learners in the audience, think of the factors in this formula as a graph. On the vertical side of the graph are the characteristics of a teen. On the horizontal line are the corresponding privileges. (See figure 4.)

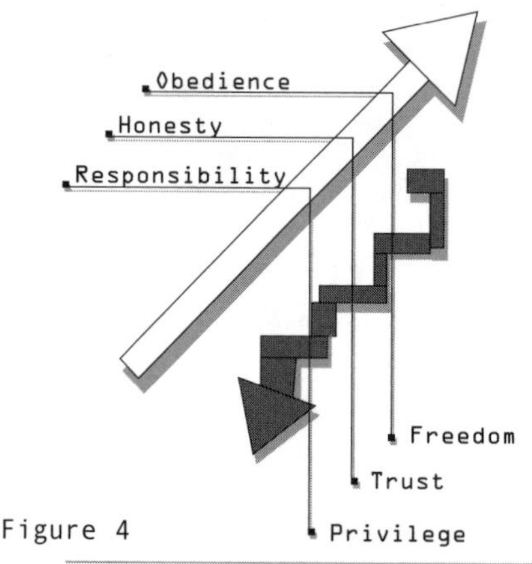

Figure 4

The ideal would be a 45-degree angle as shown.

The higher the level of responsible behavior demonstrated to parents, the more freedom a teen should earn. For instance, if a teen has a 10:00 curfew and gets home at 9:50, first the parents probably will need the services of a paramedic. But once their hearts have been restarted, they realize what a responsible teen they're harboring and probably will give him or her more freedom.

If Junior comes strolling in at 10:15, though, he goes sliding down the freedom scale like a player in the board game Chutes and Ladders.

On the Honesty-Trust line, one lie costs Junior some points. However, if Mom and Dad know whatever Junior says is "the truth, the whole truth, and nothing but the truth," he moves up the graph.

Finally, privileges usually are earned when Junior proves he is responsible.

Faith wanted pierced ears since first grade. We told her that if she would show responsibility in household chores, feeding and cleaning Cinnamon the hamster, and good personal grooming, she could have her ears pierced when she was 12. (It's not that Lois and I are that old-fashioned, we just didn't want to have to treat infected earlobes for the next five years!) Faith showed real responsibility, so on her 12th birthday, we headed to the mall for this rite of passage. (However, she slid down the scale when, at 13, she came home from summer camp with three more holes—courtesy of a friend with a safety pin!)

Freedom, trust, and privileges are not *rights*; they are earned through obedience, honesty, and responsibility. Once we've slid down one of the chutes, it's a long, hard climb back to the top.

The Eaglet Equation

The number of teens wanting out of the nest is equal to or greater than the sum total of parents struggling to let young people try their wings.

Actually, eagles have a unique way to get Junior and little sister out of the nest. For weeks, the fat little eaglets laze around the soft, down-lined nest, eating, sleeping, and gaining up to two pounds a week during eagle adolescence. Mom and Dad can't seem to keep Junior filled with fish and field mice. And little sister is demanding a room of her own.

One morning, Junior is rudely awakened by the smell of leftovers fermenting under his bed. Where's the maid? And those insensitive parents are no longer delivering food. In fact, Mom and Dad have moved out! (I am not encouraging this tactic for human parents, though it is a tempting thought at times!)

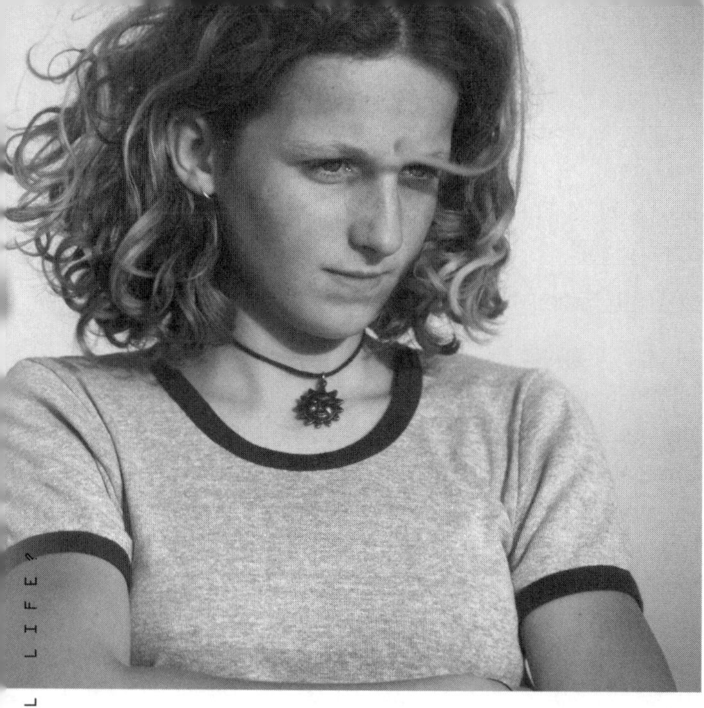

If Junior and Sister want dinner, they're going to have to get their own. And dinner is 100 feet straight down! Things were so much better in the past—no responsibilities, no hard work—Junior could have stayed home forever. Now, he's determined to leave the nest and, especially, those insensitive parents.

The eaglet totters to the edge of the nest with an odd mixture of fear, excitement, resentment, and joy. With three deep breaths, he spreads his wings and leaps into space. Actually, he tumbles and spirals toward the ground.

In folklore, suddenly Junior feels familiar feathers beneath him. It's Dad's broad wings gently lifting him out of his death dive and delivering him safely home. In the harsh reality of nature, Mom and Dad nervously watch from afar as the eaglet promptly lands on his head. Junior dusts himself off, crawls onto a rock, and attempts flight once more. This time, his wings catch the wind at just the right angle and he actually begins to gain altitude. With a fly-infested room and no more rodent pizza delivery, Junior is motivated to leave the nest and establish a life of his own.

That's a nice story, but what does it have to do with me, you ask? Read on.

My body is going through a lot of changes, but so is my attitude toward my parents. Why do they seem to irritate me so? I love them, but why do I feel so angry and talk back so much?

I believe that this seemingly universal irritation between parents and post-pubescents is the initiative for Mom and Dad to let go and for Junior to try his wings. For instance, when Faith was on the edge of the nest about to leave for Indiana Wesleyan University, she seemed especially perturbed with me. Trying to be the empathetic parent, I casually asked, "You seem kind of irritated with me. Was there anything I did to cause that?"

"Nope. It's nothing you did. You just annoy me."

Perhaps our Creator has endowed parents and teens with certain inalienable rights and among these is the right to annoy one another. Otherwise our teens would go from "whiteheads" to white heads in the nest!

But there's good news …

Watkins' Observations

1. For every misunderstood teen, there is an equally misunderstood parent.
2. Parents, who exhibit extremely low IQs when living with teens, miraculously increase in wisdom as their children grow older.
3. Parents turn into friends sometime between their kids' 18th and 22nd birthdays. (Mine did. I trust yours will too!)

The number one question in my survey of one thousand teens was "When can I start to date?"

That question has been debated since Bamm-Bamm asked Pebbles out to McDino's. And I'm sure the answer Fred and Wilma gave probably seemed prehistoric to the Flintstones' daughter. It's a tough question that is answered by even more questions.

CHAPTER

10 What's the Right Age to Start Dating?

Do You Have a Good Self-Concept?

Do you really know who you are? I mean beyond your name, address, and phone number. It's easy to lose your identity when you're dating. That's because you're trying to please the other person.

Michelle, for instance, liked the Lakers, pepperoni pizza, rap music, and the color blue when she was dating Shawn. Now that she's dating Jason, she likes the Bulls, sausage pizza, heavy metal music, and the color green. Unfortunately, not just her favorite basketball team or pizza topping has changed since dating Shawn and Jason. Her goals, dreams, values, and beliefs keep changing with each new boyfriend.

Find out who you really are—and want to be—before you start to date. And don't forget, he or she asked *you* out. Don't try to be someone else. Don't make any drastic changes in your appearance or actions. And, most important, don't change your standards just to please your date.

Do You Have Strong Self-Confidence?

A good self-concept gives you confidence. If you enjoy being with yourself, chances are that special someone will enjoy being with you as well. You don't try so hard to impress the other person if you're first impressed with yourself!

When you have a good self-concept and self-confidence, you're not so likely to be pressured into being someone else or doing something you'd rather not. (Reread chapters 4 and 5 if this is a problem.)

Do You Have Good Social Contacts?

The best dates occur between "just good friends." Here are some quick tips:

- ★ Talk about their interests, not just your own.

* ★ Brag about them, not yourself.
* ★ Be loyal to them, even when they aren't so loyal to you.
* ★ Remember, it takes real time and effort to make and keep friends.

When you date friends, you have freedom to be yourself. And you'll discover the real person, not just his or her dating image.

When can teens start going steady?

Let me suggest something that may seem right out of the town of Bedrock: Put off going steady until after high school. Here are a few practical benefits of this idea:

1. By "just being friends" with lots of guys or girls, your life will be enriched by a variety of relationships. If you go steady all through junior high and high school, you'll limit the social and emotional growth that could have occurred by having a wide range of friends.
2. There is one thing worse than not having a boyfriend or girlfriend—realizing you've had the wrong one for three years!
3. It's a lot easier to keep sexually pure if you hold off on steady relationships until later.

And that brings us to question number four:

Are You in Control Sexually?

If you answered yes, you're not ready for dating. Okay, that was a trick question, but let me explain.

Our sex drive is too powerful to control. We were created this way to make sure the human race survives. Until we realize this fact, we will have problems.

What we can control are two other factors (and they, in turn, will keep our sex drive under control): time and place. We'll talk more about this in the next chapter, but here's a sneak preview: If you limit the amount of time you spend with your date and keep out of tempting locations (empty homes and cars parked on deserted roads), your sex drive will be more likely to stay under control.

Why won't my parents let me date until I'm 17?

Maybe Mom and Dad seem a bit prehistoric because they've read a very modern report made by Brigham Young University to the Utah State Board of Education. I know that doesn't sound too exciting, but take a look at the findings: "The younger a girl is when she begins dating, the more likely it is that she will become sexually involved prematurely."[8]

Researchers found that nine out of 10 girls who began dating at age 12 became involved in premarital sex. The percentages drop dramatically for girls who began dating later. Of those who began dating at age 12, 90 percent had premarital intercourse; of those who began dating at 15, 60 percent had premarital intercourse; of those who began dating at 16, 20 percent had premarital intercourse; of those who began dating at 17, only 12 percent had premarital intercourse.

Obviously, the number of candles on your birthday cake doesn't make you more responsible or moral, but the figures do make a strong case for delaying dating until you are more mature. With maturity comes a stronger self-concept, greater self-confidence, more social contacts, and better sexual control.

So the number one question comes down to four more. Calmly discuss these with your parents to find out when is the right time for you to begin dating.

If the folks at Guinness ever decide to include the category of "World's Worst Date" in their record book, it will be either me or a character named Amnon.

To begin with, I slammed Sandy's foot in the car door, accidentally ordered anchovies on the pizza (Who wants to kiss someone with dead-fish breath?),

CHAPTER

11 How Do You Have a Great Date?

lost the car in the school parking lot, called her by the wrong name, and finally was met at the door by a blinding porch light and her six-foot-four, ex-Marine father.

Things started out better for Amnon in 2 Samuel 13:1–15. Check out this story.

> In the course of time, Amnon son of David fell in love with Tamar, the beautiful sister of Absalom son of David. (2 Samuel 13:1)

Now falling in love is great ... as long as you fall in love with the right person. It sounds harmless to say, "That person isn't really someone I'd want to spend my life with, but I'll just go out with him or her." Unfortunately, you may just find yourself feeling hopelessly in love with that person. That's why it's so important to choose ...

The Right Date

Unfortunately, Amnon wasn't listening in Sabbath school (or even reading his take-home scroll) when the class discussed Leviticus. Tamar was Amnon's half sister. Today we know one of the reasons God said no to sex with blood relatives: the chance of recessive genes coming together to produce a child who will appear on the cover of *The National Enquirer*: "Brother and sister give birth to three-eyed baby!"

But there's probably no chance that you're interested in dating your brother or sister (yeecccch)! So what do you look for? I'd suggest four things.

The Friendship Factor

Lasting love begins by being "just good friends." There is plenty of time to allow these relationships to grow. And by just being friends, you have the freedom to be yourself without the pressure of serious dating. If your date is not first your friend, he or she may be only interested in you as a body and not as a person.

The Respect Factor

Watch how this person treats other people. A good test is to see how he or she treats underclassmen or those with mental and physical handicaps. Watch how your date treats his or her family members. Does this person show disrespect for others by cutting people down behind their backs? Watch out! That person eventually will do the same to you.

The Value Factor

For a positive relationship to develop, both people need to have common values and beliefs. Without the same attitudes and priorities, any relationship is headed for Breakup City. You'll save yourself emotional pain, as well as spiritual damage, by dating only those with like beliefs. (We talked about this in chapter 7.)

The Character Factor

You don't buy a CD without first hearing the group on the radio or asking your friends if they like it. And you don't buy clothes unless you're sure your friends are wearing that style. You do some research.

In the same way, check out your possible date. Ask people who really know this person what he or she is really like. Honest or a compulsive liar? Respectful or just a people user? Accepting of others or a snob? On parole?

Don't be afraid to check this possible date out—it's a lot more important than checking out CDs and clothes.

And now back to our story.

> Amnon became frustrated to the point of illness on account of his sister Tamar, for she was a virgin, and it seemed impossible for him to do anything to her. (2 Samuel 13:2)

Is it really possible to make yourself sick by thinking about something over and over? Yep, that's why it's important to choose ...

The Right Thoughts

Ron sat in my office and squirmed in his chair. "I'm so horny, I'm gonna explode." As we talked, I discovered he had a great relationship with Keri, the best-looking girl in the youth group. Every night was a romantic, candlelight dinner, a drive up to the lookout over the Ohio River, and soft music on the radio.

But it just didn't add up to me. Everyone knew that Keri thought Ron was considered sort of a geek. After a few of my investigative reporter questions, he admitted that the relationship was only in his mind. And his thoughts went much further than soft music.

"Jim, I'm afraid I'm gonna do something crazy with all these feelings."

We can become tormented to the point of illness by our thought lives. In fact, your most powerful sexual organ isn't located where you think, but where you think—your mind! (We talked about this in chapter 5.) The right thoughts are an important part of a great date. But they're not the only part, as you'll see.

> Now Amnon had a friend named Jonadab son of Shimeah, David's brother. Jonadab was a very shrewd man. He asked Amnon, "Why do you,

the king's son, look so haggard morning after morning? Won't you tell me?"

Amnon said to him, "I'm in love with Tamar, my brother Absalom's sister."

"Go to bed and pretend to be ill," Jonadab said. "When your father comes to see you, say to him, 'I would like my sister Tamar to come and give me something to eat. Let her prepare the food in my sight so I may watch her and then eat it from her hand.'" (2 Samuel 13:3-5)

Hmmm. It sounds like Amnon may not have …

The Right Friends

Most of the advice you receive about love and dating comes from your friends. Unfortunately it's sometimes like the misinformation I got at the back of the bus one day: "Rhythm birth control is having sex while listening to the radio," Chuck announced. (He obviously hadn't read chapter 22!)

Sometimes you hear crafty advice on how to use people. Or you feel pressure to do what others are doing sexually. Like it or not, your friends and their opinions and actions have a strong impact in your life—so choose your friends carefully. As you go through adolescence, your peers' opinions will only become more and more important. They will either encourage you to keep pure or convince you that everybody is "doing it."

If you have friends now who you think may be bad influences, don't be afraid to confront them or, if you have to, drop them as friends. And don't be afraid to talk to adults you trust or to read books on the subject of sex. You need

answers to your questions, but the back of the bus or the locker room rarely provides you with the right answers. Amnon found that out the hard way.

So Amnon lay down and pretended to be ill. When the king came to see him, Amnon said to him, "I would like my sister Tamar to come and make some special bread in my sight, so I may eat from her hand."

David sent word to Tamar at the palace: "Go to the house of your brother Amnon and prepare some food for him." So Tamar went to the house of her brother Amnon, who was lying down. She took some dough, kneaded it, made the bread in his sight and baked it. Then she took the pan and served him the bread,

> but he refused to eat.
>
> "Send everyone out of here," Amnon said. So everyone left him. Then Amnon said to Tamar, "Bring the food here into my bedroom so I may eat from your hand." And Tamar took the bread she had prepared and brought it to her brother Amnon in his bedroom. (2 Samuel 13:6–10)

Did somebody say *setup?!* While you may never be in a situation quite like this (at least I hope not!), it's still a good idea to be careful about choosing …

The Right Time and Place

We talked earlier about the right time and place. The more convenient a temptation becomes, the easier it becomes to yield to it. Even if you think you're a morally strong person, it's tough to say no when you're alone together in a dimly lit room with romantic music playing in the background, or in a parked car on a deserted road, or … well, you get the point.

And the more time you spend together, the closer you grow and the more opportunities you have to get physical. So one way to hold back on physical affection is to limit the amount of time you spend alone together. Plan your outings in advance, then set an early curfew.

I know this sounds almost prehistoric, but I wish I could show you a videotape of the "good Christian teens" I've talked with. The close-ups would show the tears of disappointment, guilt, and fear they have had to deal with because they didn't plan ahead and ended up someplace they really didn't want to be.

The right place is another important part of the equation. This concept may seem Neanderthal too, but the hundreds of teens I've worked with have convinced me that dating is best done in groups or at least in semipublic places such as restaurants, ball games, church parties, parks, or the family room (as long as the rest of the family is home).

Your sex drive will stay under control much more easily if you know that at any moment Dad might walk past the family room door or that a police officer might stroll through the park.

Now, back to the story. Do you see a pattern developing? If you take the wrong date and the wrong thoughts, add the wrong friends and the wrong place, then it's unlikely you'll experience …

The Right Actions

> But when she took it to him to eat, he grabbed her and said, "Come to bed with me, my sister."
>
> "Don't, my brother!" she said to him. "Don't force me. Such a thing should not be done in Israel! Don't do this wicked thing. What about me? Where could I get rid of my disgrace? And what about you? You would be like one of the wicked fools in Israel. … But he refused to listen to her, and since he was stronger than she, he raped her.
>
> Then Amnon hated her with intense hatred. In fact, he hated her more than he had loved her. Amnon said to her, "Get up and get out!"
>
> (2 Samuel 13:11-15)
>
> So his servant put her out and bolted the door after her. She was wearing a richly ornamented robe,

> for this was the kind of garment the virgin daughters of the king wore. Tamar put ashes on her head and tore the ornamented robe she was wearing. She put her hand on her head and went away, weeping aloud as she went. (2 Samuel 13:18–19)

It's almost a mathematical equation:

Right Date
Right Thoughts
Right Friends
+ Right Time and Place
____
Right Actions

If we replace just one of the variables, we'll end up with a less-than-perfect date—and life.

But I'm hoping that if Guinness ever lists "The World's Greatest Date," you'll at least be in the top 10!

How come a guy is always supposed to pay for dates? That's not fair!

The custom of the guy paying for a date goes back thousands of years to a time when men bought their

CHAPTER

12 Who Pays?

wives. The girl's parents would hammer out a deal with the would-be husband. He would then pay 10 cows, 12 goats, and 20 chickens (or whatever the asking price was) for ownership of the girl of his dreams.

Fortunately, most of that has changed. But the idea of the man paying for dates has survived the ages.

I'd suggest sharing the costs of dating for three practical reasons:

1. Dating can get expensive. (You've probably already figured that out!)
2. Girls probably would get asked out twice as often if guys were broke half as often.

3. The best reason, though, is suggested by the question, "How come when a guy takes you someplace nice, he thinks you owe him something sexual?" As I mention throughout the book, you don't "owe" anybody your body. If you're paying for your meal and movie ticket, it's a lot less likely that the other person will lay that line on you. That way you don't owe him or her anything ... financially or sexually!

I mentioned in chapter 7 that youth camps have three things in common. Actually, there are four: pranksters with shaving cream and water balloons, teens trying to make the world's tallest human pyramid, couples in the woods … and "cling-ons." No, I'm not talking about the sworn enemies of the

CHAPTER

13 How Can I Get a Guy to Make My Life Complete?

Starship Enterprise. The cling-ons I'm referring to are teens who sit alone on the sidelines of every activity.

Since my wife and I have a real soft spot for lost puppies and cling-on teens, we make it a point to go over and talk to them. For the rest of the week, they cling to us like glue. These emotionally and socially starving people will respond to anyone who pays the least bit of attention to them.

Cling-ons come in both sexes—and are especially dangerous when they cling to another cling-on. I suspected 13-year-old Jackie was just such a person when I first met her at a youth camp. She sat by herself with a fistful of Kleenex, complaining to anyone who came within 10 feet about her terrible cold. On the other side of the cafeteria slouched Don, a 15-year-old. He, too, sat by himself with that lost-puppy look. Sure enough, they were clinging to each other before the final bonfire!

About six weeks later, I got a letter from Jackie.

> Dear Jim,
>
> Remember me from camp? I was the girl who was going with Don. Well, he lives about 50 miles away, and I just can't live without him. I'm only happy when I'm with him. I just can't wait till youth camp next year. I sent him my picture, and I've written to him, but it's not the same.
>
> I've asked my parents if we can move to his town. I just know I'll never be happy again until I am with him. Do you think you could talk to my parents? They don't want to move. But Don and I just can't live without each other. Thanks!
>
> Luv, Jackie

Lois and I usually discover that cling-ons have some serious needs. They hope "going together" will get it all together. But going together usually doesn't solve problems—it often makes them worse. (Reread that sentence. It's the most important one in this chapter.)

Don had broken up with a girl just before he met Jackie. (In fact, he had been through six "steadies" in the last year. The longest relationship had lasted two weeks.) Jackie had very few dates before she met Don. But now they were sure that this was the relationship that would meet all their needs.

We've tried to help such couples see that

Going Together Doesn't Get It Together Emotionally

As I talked with Jackie and Don, I discovered two insecure people with little respect for themselves. They were expecting steady dating to improve their self-worth.

Why is it so painful when you really care for a person and want to be with him or her, but one of you is always busy with school, work, parents, etc.?

If your self-worth is shaky before going together, it will be rocked in a "steady" situation. Unthinking remarks by your partner about the way you look, talk, dress, bowl, roller-skate, kiss, and so on can damage a weak sense of self-worth. So work on developing your self-worth before you start to date.

Jackie particularly was sure that one week of camp would cure a lifetime of painful loneliness. But if you are lonely before Mr. or Ms. Right comes along, it probably will get worse after a few weeks of dating. He or she will not want to spend every waking hour with you. He or she will still have friends to do things with. So find out the cause of your loneliness before you say yes to a steady proposal.

Both Jackie and Don were longing for emotional intimacy. But if you don't have any really close friendships now, it's doubtful that going together will create such a relationship. Work at being vulnerable and open with a friend of the same sex before you try to develop emotional intimacy with the opposite sex—and they are opposite in many ways!

Going Together Doesn't Get It Together Socially

One of the worst things camp directors do is schedule a "dress-up banquet" for the last night of camp. All week guys agonize over finding a girl to take to this major social event. And if by Thursday you don't have a date, you might as well hang a sign around your neck that says "Camp Geek."

Jackie and Don may have been cling-ons, but at least they didn't have to face the humiliation of sitting by themselves Friday night.

At school, too, some teens go steady simply because of peer pressure or the status they receive by going with someone. But don't let others' expectations force you into a relationship just for status. That's using your steady for selfish reasons. And a relationship based on what the other can do for you won't last long.

Going Together Doesn't Get It Together Sexually

Some cling-ons just want to cling on sexually. (We'll talk more about that in chapter 20.) A couple may get sexual release out of a relationship, but they may also get something worse. (We'll talk about *that* in chapter 22.)

Going Together Doesn't Get It Together Spiritually

We've talked to couples who have clung to each other without realizing the need was really spiritual. "Maybe going together will fill that emptiness I feel," Jackie confided in another letter.

I tried to share with her that going steady—or even a great marriage—won't fill that God-shaped vacuum in your soul. Only faith in Christ can bring deep, satisfying fulfillment. (If you haven't experienced this for yourself, be sure to reread the end of chapter 7.)

Going steady requires two emotionally, socially, and spiritually whole individuals. Both partners encourage each other's potential development, and each becomes a better person. (You may want to reread chapter 7 where we talked about what it takes to build a solid relationship.)

Listed below are some differences between those who "cling on" and those who "lift up" their boyfriends or girlfriends.

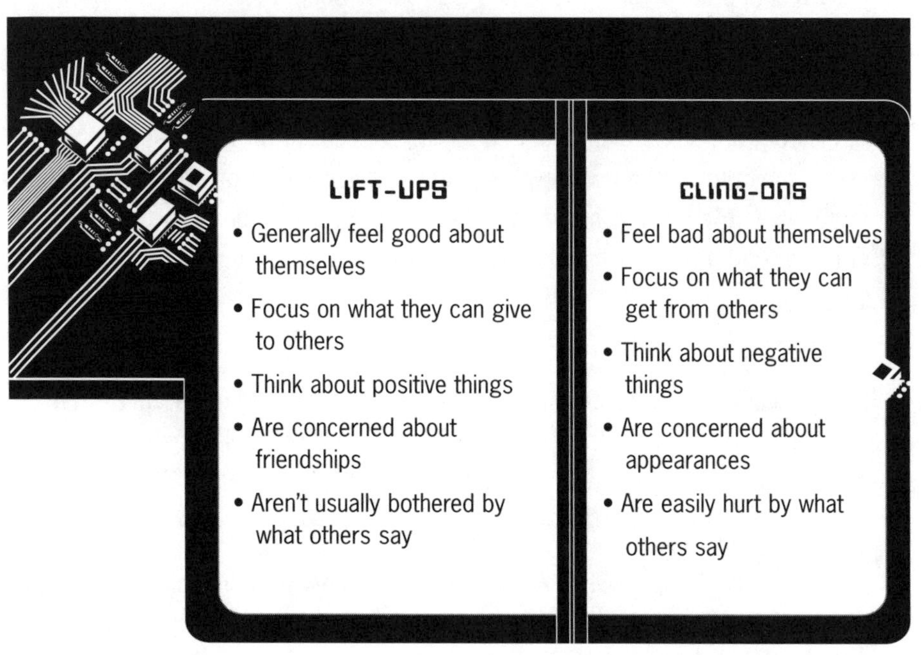

LIFT-UPS	CLING-ONS
• Generally feel good about themselves	• Feel bad about themselves
• Focus on what they can give to others	• Focus on what they can get from others
• Think about positive things	• Think about negative things
• Are concerned about friendships	• Are concerned about appearances
• Aren't usually bothered by what others say	• Are easily hurt by what others say

Going together, then, isn't the solution to problems. It isn't two emotional cripples trying to hold each other up. It isn't two half-people attempting to make a whole life. In fact, if, like Jackie and Don, you just *have* to go together, exchanging class rings is not the answer.

"I've gotta talk to you right after tonight's youth meeting," I stammered.

"I've gotta talk to you too," my girlfriend replied.

That's all we said for the rest of the meeting. We held hands during the whole session, but it was mostly out of force of habit. We walked silently into a deserted classroom and just sat there trying not to look at each other.

Finally, I pulled her class ring off my little finger and

CHAPTER 14

How Do You Know If You Should Break Up with Somebody?

handed it to her. She unpinned my Quill and Scroll award from her sweater and handed it to me.

"I'm sorry, Sandy." "Me too, Jim."

Then we silently walked out of the room and out of each other's lives.

Neither of us was really sure why we were breaking up. Maybe it was because I'd be leaving for an out-of-state college soon, and we knew that long-distance relationships rarely worked. Maybe we had just grown apart during our year and a half of steady dating. Or perhaps we were too much alike. Who knew? We just both realized that something very precious to us both was over.

Should you break up with someone, even if you still like him a lot?

Since my breakup with Sandy, many teens have asked me, "When and how do you break up?" Each relationship is different, but these general principles may help.

Know When to Break Up

It's time to call it quits when

1. You can't be yourself with your partner.
2. You feel that the relationship is smothering you emotionally, socially, or spiritually. (Remember the cling-ons from the last chapter?)

3. You sense there are differences in values, beliefs, and life goals. (Reread chapter 7 if you feel you're in an unstable relationship.)
4. One of you is moving a long distance away. Looking back, both Sandy and I would have missed rich opportunities to get to know other people if we had tried to keep up a 150-mile relationship for several years. As soon as I left, she started to date one of my good friends. It took me longer to start dating seriously again, but then I met my wife-to-be.
5. You find yourself outgrowing the person. I really believed we were right for each other during the time Sandy and I were together, but we were growing in different directions.
6. You're in an emotionally, physically, or sexually abusive relationship. Don't make excuses for your partner—just get out!

Here are some poor reasons for breaking up.

1. You disagree. Relationships that can withstand a real disagreement now and then stand a better chance of surviving. Unless the disagreement involves one of the foundation levels of the interpersonal pyramid we talked about in chapter 7, work at understanding each other.
2. The "old feelings" fade. Feelings are certainly important, but we can't build a lasting relationship on them. Reread chapter 6 if you sense you've lost the feeling. Plenty of *agape* may be left—you may just experience a decrease in *eros*.
3. You're married. The principles in this chapter are for steady or engaged relationships. I'm definitely not suggesting a wife call a divorce lawyer if she feels the relationship with her husband is growing apart. Even in abusive situations, I'd only suggest a temporary separation. During that "time-out," I would encourage the couple to seek

professional counseling and work to restore the relationship.

Know How to Break Up

1. Break up in person. Don't be a coward and write him or her a letter. It's much healthier emotionally to end the relationship face-to -face.
2. Break up cleanly. Don't dredge up everything that has been wrong with the relationship. Simply tell him or her that you don't feel that your relationship should continue as it is.
3. Break up clearly. Is this a temporary breakup to think things through, then talk things out? Is this a change in the relationship rather than an end? For instance, do you still want to date this person but also have the freedom to date other people? Is this good-bye forever?

Don't play guessing games or expect your partner to read your mind. I wish Sandy and I would have talked more after our breakup. At the time I hurt so much I didn't even want to see her—even though we attended the same church and sang on the same TV program.

Finally, a year later, we wrote several long letters to each other that helped each of us understand what had happened. What a relief to discover that we both valued those 18 months and could still be friends!

Breaking up does hurt—a lot! We've already talked about the emotional bonding that develops in relationships (in chapter 6). It's like an old Elmer's Glue commercial. Two blocks of wood are glued together. Then two bulldozers pull the glued blocks apart. The bond is still in good shape, but the wood has splintered. "Elmer's Glue—stronger than the wood itself," the announcer claims. In the same way, it is impossible to break a bond without causing a lot of pain in the process!

But breaking up doesn't have to mean breaking down. Try to see how you grew and what you learned through the relationship. Sandy gave me back my honor society pin, but she kept those 18 months of my life. I gave her school ring back. But I kept a year and a half of concerts, youth meetings, milk shakes, school banquets, television productions, valentine cards, dinners at Ponderosa and Burger King, long talks, dreams, and hopes. Most of all, we kept things that would last the rest of our lives: emotional openness, social confidence, and spiritual growth. We've remained in contact throughout the years and can now look back on our going together as a positive part of our lives.

That's an important point to remember. In each relationship from Sandy to my wife, Lois, I have become a more caring, more honest, more understanding person. (That's what girls teach us "insensitive jerks.") With each date and each serious relationship, we learn invaluable lessons about others and ourselves.

One hit song of the '60s cries, "Breaking up is hard to do." That's true—but there's one thing worse: staying together with the wrong person!

Part FOUR

What's Happening to Me Sexually?

There would be some real advantages if we were all one gender. Clothing would only have to button one way. No more arguments about women in the military. No more sexual discrimination or harassment. And best of all, we wouldn't have to argue about in what position to leave the toilet seat or whether to

CHAPTER

15

What's the Reason for Sex besides Having Kids?

stop for directions.

However, there are some real advantages to sexual differences that go beyond the charts in sixth-grade health class. For instance, if you came home from the hospital in a blue blanket, you'll tend to solve problems, think, and relate to others in generally one way. If your blanket was pink, you'll probably solve problems, think, and relate to others in a very different way.

Our biology causes many of these differences—things like estrogen and testosterone levels.

Others are the result of how and where we were raised. For instance, we would think and act differently if we had grown up in an African tribe where the women were the leaders and men cared for the children ("Your husband is certainly a great little hut-keeper."). And we would think and act differently if we were raised in a Middle Eastern country where women are treated like men's property ("I'll give you 50 sheep and 25 goats for your daughter, sir." "Throw in a camel and you've got yourself a deal, son.").

How come girls are so weird?

Why are guys such jerks?

To put it in computer terms, sexuality is more than having male or female hardware. And there's much more to sex than networking computer mainframes. We need the opposite sex for some very good reasons, including mental, social, and spiritual upgrades in our software.

We Need the Opposite Sex for Mental Growth

Women

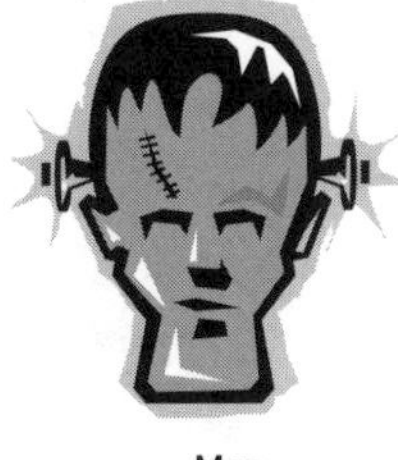

Men

There are very real differences between male and female thinking. Research on stroke victims has revealed that men's and women's brains are physically distinct—differences that often make women seem "spacey" and men appear thickheaded.

Here's how it works. If we were to look at an embryo at the 12th week of life, we would see a distinct human being; it would even have fingernails. And, on closer inspection, we would say, "Look, it's a girl!" But it could very well be a boy!

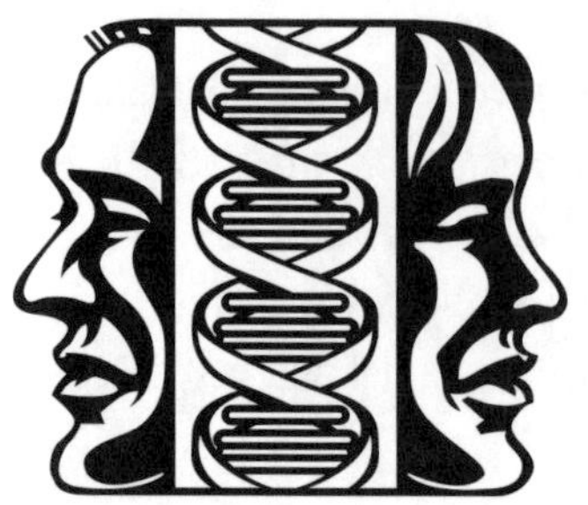

The gender of a fetus is determined at the split second of conception: An "X" sperm outraces a "Y" sperm to the egg and we have a female; a "Y" sperm beats the others to the egg and we have a male. But the fetus will look female until the chromosomes—the genetic blueprint—call for male hormones to be produced. The androgen will slowly transform the previously "female" fetus into a perfectly formed—and anatomically correct—male.

But that's not all. In the 16th week, another dose of androgen begins to transform the "XY" fetus' brain from female to male. Many of the nerve connections between the two sides dissolve. And the sides, or hemispheres, of the male brain begin to take on different jobs. Because of this, guys can only use half a brain at a time. But women can use both sides of their brain at the same time.

Females also can store information in both sides of their brain. They "back up" all their information. Men can't. That's why a stroke is usually more damaging to a man. A certain "disk sector" of his brain has been wiped out, and he has no backup disk.

The research also seems to say that most females are dominated by the left, or verbal side, and most males by the right, or visual side. (So we men may only use half a brain, but we're at least in our "right" minds!) For instance, have you ever heard this dialogue?

Male: "Tell me how you came to that conclusion."

Female: "I don't know. I just knew it."

Male: "Come on. You just can't have answers pop into your head. How did you figure that out?"

Female: "Well, I just knew it."

The woman may not be able to explain logically, step by step the thinking that instantly came to the correct answer. Her brain simply has better wiring with information firing back and forth between the hemispheres!

Now don't feel too superior, ladies. There are some advantages to only using half a brain at one time. Boys seem to be better in logical problem solving and higher math in school. Because girls have more nerve connections between the halves of their brains, they can handle both visual and verbal information at the same time. Thus, they often talk earlier than boys and generally do better in language arts.[9]

So males and females are born not only physically different, but mentally different as well. And that can cause all kinds of communication problems or it can enrich our lives (usually both). If we want a 3-D, stereophonic view of life, we need to know how the opposite sex sees and hears the world. If we refuse, we might as well listen to only one side of the headphones or watch a 3-D movie with one eye closed.

A year ago I couldn't stand guys. Now I can't stand not being with them. Why is that?

How come I used to hate girls and now I just have to be around them?

Sexual differences allow us to look at our world from different viewpoints and to learn from the other gender's perspective.

We Need the Opposite Sex for Social Growth

Ancient marriage counselors believed that human beings originally came in just one gender. Things went along wonderfully well without the aforementioned

arguments over toilet seats and stopping for directions. But the gods, who were often in bad moods, became angry with the whole human race.

"What's the worst punishment we can inflict on these creatures? Ravaging rashes, continuous constipation, or tenacious telemarketers?" After much drinking, debating, and more drinking, the gods thought up a rather creative torture:

"Let's cut each human in two, shuffle them up, and deal them out across the face of the earth. Then, we'll sit back and watch these frustrated creatures try to find their other half!" (The Latin word *sexus* means "to split.")

I have to admit that I didn't feel the effects of this ancient curse in grade school. Girls never did anything interesting during recess. Sometimes they jumped rope, but mostly they just stood around giggling. They dressed Barbie dolls when they could have been throwing rocks at one another or hanging by one knee from the monkey bars.

The only girl worth knowing in elementary school was Val (she hated being called Valerie). And she was one mean football player. I liked her, and she had a great dirt bike. Mostly, though, girls were to be avoided at all costs. (This was during one of history's worst "cooties" outbreaks and, of course, girls were the primary carriers.)

Girls were still pretty "dumb" in junior high. They never did anything interesting during lunch break. They just stood around giggling—they didn't even play with Barbie dolls. (Actually, I learned later they were laughing at us "totally immature" boys!)

Then I discovered puberty and Karen! She didn't play football or even have a dirt bike, but there was this strange, almost painful attraction. I found myself plotting ways to sit next to her on the bus. I was ecstatic when I discovered we had three classes together. And, of course, she acted like I didn't exist!

But I discovered that as we interact with the opposite sex, we learn new social skills. Guys who once prided themselves in passing gas and belching out "The National Anthem" actually can learn to eat with utensils and say "please" and "thank you." We also can be trained—at least theoretically—in other social skills such as showing feelings and being sensitive to others by watching women act and react to others. Women can learn to be more assertive and to take things less personally by being around men.

Why are guys so insensitive? They don't care how others feel!

Why are girls so oversensitive? They take everything so personally!

I have to admit that I was a total jerk before I met Lois. Okay, I'll probably die a jerk, but I have seen a lot of changes in the way I treat people after dating and now being married to her for more than 25 years. And I think Lois has learned to be willing to take risks—like living with a freelance writer—and not to take things as personally because she's lived with me for so long.

Sexuality, then, is not merely a physical need. And even as a drive, it isn't that strong. We can't survive without food, water, and oxygen, but we can live quite well without intercourse. (I've never seen an obituary listing the cause of death as "coital deprivation syndrome.")

What's more, intercourse is the only biological drive that needs another person for normal expression. We can breathe, eat, and drink alone, but satisfying intercourse requires a close social relationship. That's why taking things into your own hands (we'll talk about that in chapter 17) and pornography are so unsatisfying. It's hard to have meaningful dialogue with a picture or a video image! And there's no mental growth, which a relationship with a real, flesh-and-blood person offers. It's even harder to have a social life with a centerfold. We don't grow socially when our only close contact with the opposite sex is people with staples through their navels. That's why people addicted to pornography tend to withdraw into their own world and slowly die mentally and socially. Or they turn to "cyber sex," which at least offers keyboarded conversation.

But social relationships take time to develop. In an age of microwave popcorn, we expect social needs to be met instantly as well. Unfortunately, real social growth doesn't happen in four to five minutes on "high heat."

We Need the Opposite Sex for Spiritual Growth

We had a really cool flip chart in sixth-grade health class made of transparent sheets. You could peel the skin right off the poor character to reveal his muscles. Another flip of the chart exposed all his internal organs. A final flip and there were his spine and kidneys.

What the chart didn't show was what makes us unique human beings. Sure, we're all carbon-based life-forms with 46 chromosomes, but below our pectoralis majors, sternums, right atriums, and tricuspid valves—even deeper—is something that gives us our spiritual heart and soul. Our dreams, our creativity, our ways of thinking and perceiving life, our sense of who we are and how we fit into creation can't be seen with X-rays.

Part of our personality can be explained by heredity and our passions can be attributed to hormones. But the majority of what makes me "me" and you

"you"—in the deepest and most intimate way—is beyond reach of scientific study.

Sexuality not only reveals our physical and mental differences, but on an even deeper level our spiritual differences.

Why are girls so hard to figure out?

Why are guys so hard to understand?

And for people of faith, there is an even more remarkable—and dare I say "sacred"—aspect of sexuality. In the story of creation, God creates male and female "in His own image" (Genesis 1:27). So here's my theory: God's image is so wonderfully complex that He had to make two genders to fully express who He is.

All of a sudden my faith seems shaken by lots of questions. What's happening?

Perhaps the reason God appears contradictory at times is that He is expressing His more feminine side. He speaks of Himself as a "mother hen gathering her chicks." He refers to Himself as "El Shaddai," which is translated "the one which nourishes," but the Hebrew root word also can be translated "the breast"! At other times, we see a more masculine side complete with lightning bolts, plagues, and fire from heaven.

Those nights that I'm wide awake at 3 A.M., I wonder, Did God give us the wonderfully complex opposite sex to help us understand His wonderfully complex personality? I'll never fully understand God—or Lois—but I love them both dearly. And both have enriched my life in ways that couldn't have occurred individually.

Finally, throughout both the Old and New Testaments, God uses sexuality as a symbol for the spiritual closeness He wants to have with His creation. What's the Hebrew male's symbol of commitment to his God? Circumcision! For Christians, St. Paul says that a marriage is a human "symbol" of the union of Christ and His bride, the Church (see Ephesians 5:31–32).

Sexuality, then, reminds me that I'm incomplete—physically, mentally (no doubt there!), and spiritually. It forces me from being a self-centered, sexist pig to realizing that I am in need of others. And, remarkably, that others need me to be a complete person. It also reminds me that I am "fearfully and wonderfully made" (Psalm 139:14) by a very creative, loving God.

Amazing!

Rock stars dress up in makeup and women's clothing. Picketers outside the funeral of a homosexual hold up signs proclaiming, "God hates fags." Schools offer "sensitivity" classes to promote the idea that gay and lesbian lifestyles should be accepted as normal. Talk shows are filled with

CHAPTER 16

Why Am I So Confused about Who I Am Sexually?

homosexual guests as well as transsexuals, bisexuals, and transvestites.

No wonder several students wrote on my survey, "Why am I so confused about who I am sexually?" and "Why is God so bent out of shape about homosexuality?"

Why do we make a big deal about whether we're male or female?

Let's begin at the beginning. The very beginning. God's very image is expressed in the marriage relationship between a man and woman. (We talked about that in the previous chapter.)

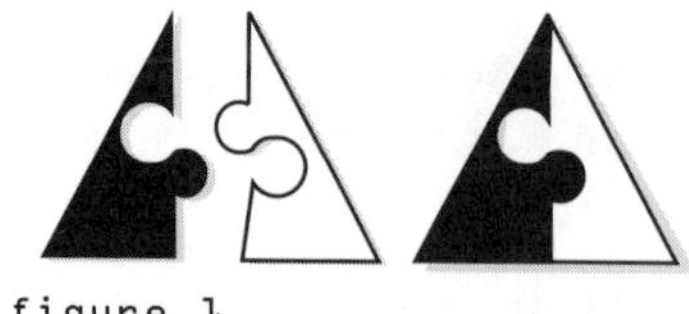
figure 1

If we visualize God as a triangle, figure 1 illustrates how both genders—male and female—are necessary to fully express God's character.

God's very image is distorted in a union between the same sexes. Notice in figure 2 that two male parts of the triangle and two female parts of the triangle, no matter how they are arranged, do not make a complete image of God.

figure 2

Why is God so bent out of shape by homosexual behavior?

Perhaps God gets so bent out of shape over homosexual behavior because His very image is bent out of shape.

With that in mind, let's talk about some theories of why between 1 and 10 percent of Americans consider themselves homosexual.

Jesus seems to *imply* that there are several possible reasons people may not have normal relations with the opposite sex: "Some are born without the ability to marry, and some are disabled by men, and some refuse to marry for the sake of the kingdom of heaven" (Matthew 19:12 TLB).

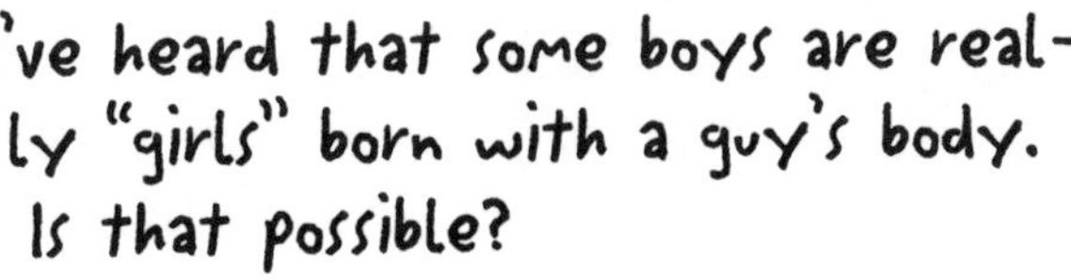

I've heard that some boys are really "girls" born with a guy's body. Is that possible?

"Some Are Born"

In the previous chapter, we talked about how "male" and "female" bodies and brains develop in the womb. (At 12 weeks, a blast of androgen transforms a female-looking fetus into an anatomically correct male. At 16 weeks, another dose of the hormone dissolves many of the connections between the hemispheres of a male brain. So males and females are very different physically and mentally.)

So confusion over sexual identity may be a result of a birth defect. Say, for instance, a male fetus gets a dose of androgen at 12 weeks. It would develop into a perfectly formed boy. But what would happen if for some reason it didn't get the second dose of androgen? It would have a male body but a female brain. Some people believe this is a possible cause for sexual confusion.

Some people consider themselves "androgynous," meaning they have both female and male characteristics in one body. For instance, a rock star told *Rolling Stone* magazine, "I'm as gay as I am heterosexual. I don't believe people should be defined by their sexuality. I'm not particularly masculine, and I'm not particularly feminine. I don't think it matters."[10]

A study at Johns Hopkins also has revealed that many girls who are labeled tomboys have higher levels of androgen. And at UCLA they discovered that women who took male hormones for pregnancy problems had girls who thought and fought like guys.

However, there's not conclusive evidence to prove homosexuals are born "that way." There is, however, much evidence to indicate ...

"Some Are Disabled by Men"

Confusion over sexual identity also may be the result of upbringing.

Why do I feel the same about guys as I do about girls?

Hormones don't lock us into male or female behavior. They just make it easier to act like one or the other. In fact, most research seems to show that our upbringing is more powerful than our genes when it comes to sexual identity.

Those born with confused hormones can grow up perfectly normal if they are brought up with good role models and lots of love. But a biologically "perfect" individual can have homosexual tendencies if he or she is brought up with poor role models, abuse, or incest.

Silly Ideas of What God Was Like

The apostle Paul seems to add a third reason for sexual confusion:

> Yes, they knew about [God] all right, but they wouldn't admit it or worship Him or even thank Him for all His daily care. And after awhile they began to think up silly ideas of what God was like and what He wanted them to do. The result was that their foolish minds became dark and confused. ... That is why God let go of them and let them do

> all these evil things, so that even their women turned against God's natural plan for them and indulged in sex sin with each other. And the men, instead of having a normal sex relationship with women, burned with lust for each other, men doing shameful things with other men and, as a result, getting paid within their own souls with the penalty they so richly deserved.
>
> (Romans 1:21, 26–27 TLB)

If we go back to our triangle illustrations, we can see that when we totally reject God, we often reject His created purposes for male and female relationships.

So the Bible seems to imply that there are three possible reasons for sexual dysfunctions: biology, upbringing, and rejection of God. (Unfortunately, there's no chapter in the Bible that specifically addresses all these issues. We're left to piece together clues.)

If you can't help but have gay feelings, why does God condemn you for something you can't help?

God never condemns the individual with a confused sexual identity. It may have been completely out of the individual's control. God loves us regardless of our sexual inclinations. But He also hates actions that are destructive to our physical and emotional well-being.

For instance, raise your hand if you consider yourself heterosexual (having an attraction to the opposite gender). Okay, that's most of you. Now, does that give you the right to have sex with anyone of the opposite sex? I mean, after all, you were born heterosexual or taught a heterosexual orientation! Of course not. That's part of living responsibly and according to God's plan.

Throughout Scripture, God points out how destructive homosexual behavior can become. Just check out Leviticus 18:22; 20:13; Romans 1:22–29; 1 Corinthians 6:9—20; and Jude 7. But with God's power and an understanding counselor, a person with sexual confusion can find help. It may not change his or her inclinations, but it can help him or her act responsibly.

The Bible is also clear that homosexual acts are *not* unforgivable sins. In fact the church in Corinth was filled with members who once were "sexually immoral ... adulterers ... male prostitutes ... [and] homosexual offenders" who had been "washed ... sanctified ... [and] justified in the name of the Lord Jesus Christ and by the Spirit of our God" (1 Corinthians 6:9–11).

How do you tell if you're homosexual or bisexual or what? Sometimes I wonder if I am.

It's also important to separate feelings of sexual confusion with actual homosexual orientation. More than one third of all guys and many girls go through a temporary time of sexual confusion. But according to Dr. Wayne Oates, a psychiatry professor at the University of Louisville, that does not mean that you're homosexual. And homosexuality doesn't refer to "the fear of being homosexual, to fantasies of homosexual behavior, or to (occasional) events of homosexual behavior, particularly in the early and pre-adult years."[11]

Dr. Oates claims that "homosexual refers to a person who has, after adulthood, chosen consciously and decided clearly that he or she wants to gain sexual satisfaction from persons of the same sex."[12]

What should I do if another guy wants me to have sex with him?

Just because you have confusing sexual feelings at this time doesn't mean you're a homosexual. Some adult homosexuals will try to convince you that you are. "Well, if you have those feelings, you must be gay. So why fight it?"

Don't believe them. In fact, the Allan Gutmacher Institute recently discovered that only about 1 percent of the population is truly homosexual.

You're not alone in your feelings. If you have concerns, talk about it with somebody you can trust.

Rick shifted in the office chair and twisted the spiral on his notebook.

"I'm having a real struggle with this … habit. I've prayed about it and really tried to stop, but I still do it. I mean, it's really embarrassing."

He paused to stare out the window, then continued.

CHAPTER

17 Will It Really Make You Go Crazy?

"I know I shouldn't and I just know it would kill my folks if they knew I was … I've never talked to anyone about it … well, it's just embarrassing."

He stared out the window once more.

"Does it begin with the letter *M*, Rick?" I asked as our eyes finally met.

"Yeah, but how did you know?!"

Rick was the fourth person that month to admit to me that masturbation was a problem. (Masturbation is rubbing your penis or vaginal area to receive pleasure and orgasm.) There's a good chance you, too, may be struggling with this issue. Ninety-eight percent of men and over one third of women are struggling or have struggled with this hidden habit, yet very few are willing to discuss it.

Are you gay if you "play with yourself"?

Will masturbation keep you from having kids?

Occasional masturbation is a part of exploring and experimenting with newly developing sexual drives for young teens. Research has shown that occasional masturbation causes no ill effects—physically or mentally. It won't keep you from having children, make hair grow on your palms, or drain off all your energy. And it won't make you crazy! (The mentally ill often masturbate more because they are mentally ill. They are not mentally ill because they often masturbate.)

Why did God give me these feelings and drives when it's so long until marriage?

Masturbation has become a much larger issue in modern society. Two hundred years ago, a 14-year-old boy and a 12-year-old girl could support themselves by farming. In modern society, couples are delaying marriage for educational and financial reasons, so the age at which people marry has been delayed dramatically—more than ten years!

At the same time, the age of sexual maturity has dropped this century from age 18 to around 13 for girls and

15 for boys. For African American girls, the age has dropped to as low as 8.

Masturbation was never an issue when one married before sexual maturity. Today, the time from sexual maturity to marriage has increased to 10 or more years. So masturbation becomes one way to deal with these trends.

However, there is much confusion, guilt, and insecurity when masturbation becomes a regular practice. As a habit, it often creates feelings of guilt, shame, and sometimes worthlessness. It causes some people to become withdrawn and insecure.

Masturbation, however, loses its humiliating and guilt-producing feelings when we can discuss our feelings with a trusted adult or counselor. (I think the number of guys who stopped by to discuss the issue was motivated by the word getting out: "You can talk to Jim about this and he won't freak out.") Hidden fears, desires, and temptations cause us the most problems.

Here are some danger signs that masturbation is becoming a problem.

1. Masturbation becomes a substitute for healthy friendships or emotional intimacy with others. If you're becoming withdrawn from others or feel you don't need others because of it, you probably need to discuss the problem with a trusted adult or a professional counselor.
2. Masturbation becomes a substitute for intercourse in marriage. Sex is designed to communicate love and intimacy with your spouse. Stimulating yourself doesn't. In fact, it's really not sexual stimulation at all, but simply self-stimulation. Licensed marriage counselors are trained to deal with this issue.
3. Masturbation becomes an uncontrollable habit or you find yourself masturbating in public places. It's definitely time for some professional help.

Is it wrong to make yourself have an orgasm?

Is masturbation a sin?

For people of faith, there are additional questions. What does God say about masturbation? Is it a sin? Unfortunately, the Bible says absolutely nothing about self-stimulation. (It would be much easier to deal with the issue if there was a verse that said, "Thou shalt not" or "Verily, verily, it's okay.") So why doesn't God say anything about it? Possibly because it was not an issue in ancient times for reasons we've already discussed. Possibly because God really doesn't care whether you occasionally masturbate. God's Word *does* have a lot to say about our thought life and our moral behavior.[13]

So masturbation is not physically or mentally damaging, but if it's causing sufficient anxiety in your life, talk to a trained professional. Most of all, remember you're not alone in this hidden habit.

The sports car races down the track toward the announcer, who is standing with his back to the car. He calmly talks about the dependability of the car: the responsive steering, the solid handling, the road-hugging control, and, we all hope, the reliable brakes! Then, just before the announcer becomes a

CHAPTER

18 How Far Is Too Far?

hood ornament, the car screeches to a stop … only inches from his back.

"We not only stand behind our cars, we stand in front of them," the man proclaims.

It's a great commercial. Unfortunately, we humans are not designed with that kind of control—or those kinds of brakes—when it comes to sexual expression.

Many teens with good morals believe they can aim their dating behavior toward intercourse, floor the accelerator, and come screeching to a stop just inches before they go too far. Unfortunately, they often discover that those brakes no longer work, and they end up crashing into the concrete wall of reality.

So what is a safe distance?

How far is too far on a date?

Before we answer that, let's ask another question: What is the purpose of physical expression? Is it a thank-you for dinner and a concert? Is it something to do on a date? Is it "making love"?

The answers are: No. No. And especially no. Physical contact *expresses* love, it never *makes* love. That's why physical expression should never go farther than the love itself.

Do you think it's all right to do a lot of sexual things if you really love the person?

Let's picture this as a graph. On the vertical side is the expression of affection—from holding hands to going **"all the way."** On the horizontal plane is the level of commitment—from the first date to marriage.

Chart 1 shows one couple's expression of affection compared to commitment.

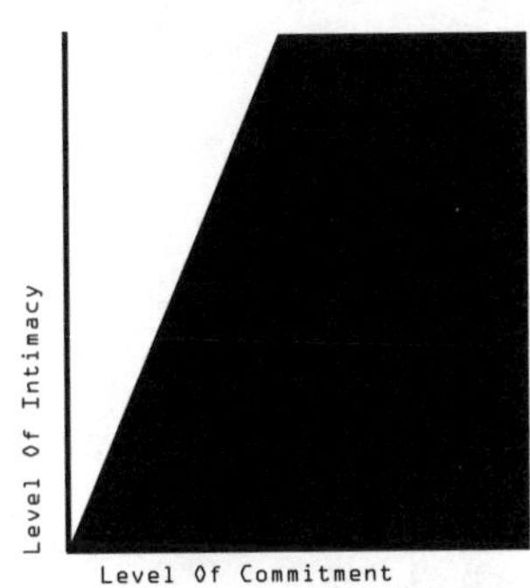

Chart 1

Eric asks Marian out to Burger King for a shake. Marian is flattered and wants to be asked out again. So she allows Eric to hold her hand. For a shake and movie, he expects a goodnight kiss. If he takes Marian out to a restaurant that doesn't have a drive-up window, he expects some serious hugging and kissing. And so it continues.

Eric says, “I really like you,” thus moving him half an inch on the commitment line. Marian is so thrilled, she allows him to move three inches up the intimacy line. “I love you” moves the couple three inches on the commitment line and half a yard on the physical affection line.

Soon Eric and Marian have gone farther than they intended, but they're convinced they love each other. So when either begins to doubt the other's love, they increase the physical affection in hopes that it will increase the level of commitment. They try to maintain love by “making love.” But because there is more sex than love, Eric and Marian both feel empty and used. They don't realize that they can't make love through physical affection, they can only express the love that's already there.

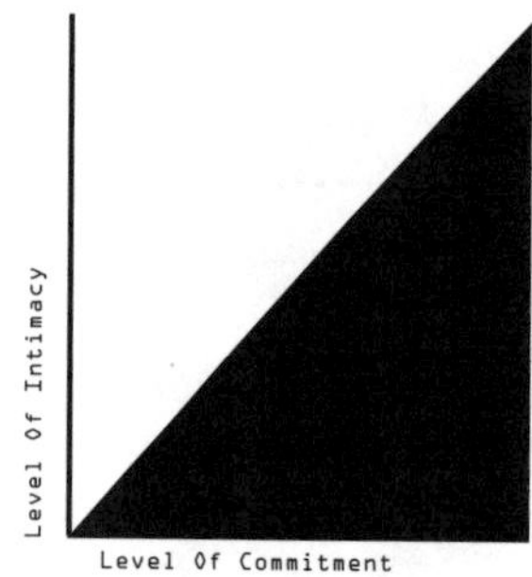

Chart 2

Chart 2 shows the ideal.

Let's back up and get Eric and Marian on track. As they move down the commitment line, they move the same distance up the intimacy line. This is what gives physical affection its meaning—holding hands, hugging, and kissing express a relationship.

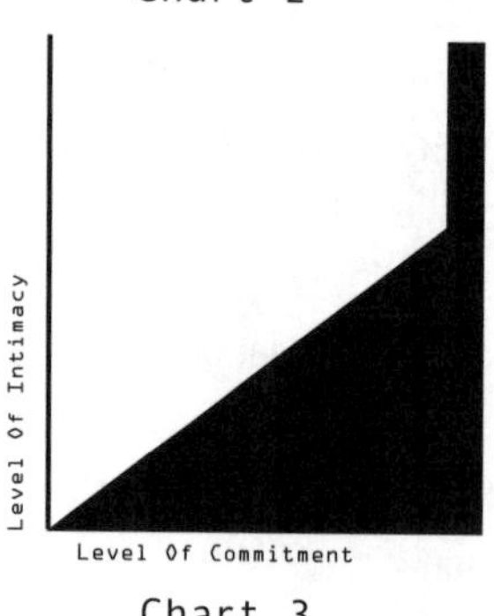

Chart 3

But the ideal is just ideal. Our bodies have a built-in **"point of no return."** Once it is crossed, virtually all will have sexual intercourse. That point, unfortunately, is different in different people. And it is unknown.

The safest plan, then, is to keep well below the point where you sense your brakes slipping. That's why I suggest chart 3.

Let's go back to the sports car commercial. The announcer is probably safe inside a TV studio. Behind him is a green wall—not a speeding car. The engineer simply runs a videotape of the car and track, blends it with the footage of the announcer and—wow!—the thrilling effect.

We also need to stay in the area of safety. Again, this is why I would suggest controlling the time you spend and places you go with your date. (Okay, okay, I've already said that three times in this book, but it's important!)

Remember that physical affection should never be greater than your level of commitment. If you're not ready for the legal and emotional commitments of marriage, then you're not ready for intercourse. Marriage provides intercourse with security—you don't have to worry about getting caught or getting pregnant. It creates meaning—you have never done this with anyone else. It's the ultimate physical expression of your love for each other. And that's how God intended it: as the ultimate demonstration of love between a husband and wife.

So until you have a driver's license, it's a good idea to stay off the road. And until you have a marriage license, it's a good idea to stay off deserted roads.

What should Marian, whom we met in the last chapter, do if Eric wants to go further than she does? (And it's not only girls who are at risk for sexual assault. While one out of three girls from ages 15 to 24 will experience some kind of sexual assault, one out of eight guys in that age group will as well.)

Here are some proven ways to greatly reduce the risk.

CHAPTER 19

What If a Date Won't Respect Your Limits?

What should you do if you're on a date and the date wants to have sex and you don't want to?

1. Know your date. Never leave a party or some other event with someone you've just met! (Always have your own transportation or plans for a ride before going to an event.)
2. Know you have the right to set sexual limits. You may have different limits with different people; your limits may change over time. It's a good idea to know what you

want and don't want before you end up in the backseat of a car or in an empty house.

3. Let your date know your limits. Get them across to the other person verbally—ESP doesn't work—and be sure the person knows your limits aren't adjustable. And don't confuse your date by sending out mixed signals. Do your clothing, body language, and physical expressions say no? Or is your attire or posture saying yes? Do your music and movie choices celebrate premarital sex? (Don't go to an R-rated movie if you don't want R-rated moves.)
4. Stay in public places (stadium, movie complex, concert venue, restaurant, etc.) or in a group, especially if you're on your first few dates.
5. Trust your feelings. If you feel you are being pressured into unwanted sex, you're probably right. Act on your feelings and get out of the situation as calmly and as quickly as possible.

I'd like to date, but I'm afraid of getting raped. How do you know what a guy has on his mind?

6. Pay attention to behavior that doesn't seem right. Some warning signs are

★ Someone who is rude, lewd, or crude. If you're not shocked, he or she may think you're actually interested in what's being talked about.

★ Someone standing too close who seems to enjoy your discomfort.

★ Someone who stares at you or seems to be looking through or down at you.

★ Someone who purposely blocks your way.

★ Someone speaking or acting as if he or she knows you more intimately than he or she does.

★ Someone who grabs or pushes you to get his or her way.

★ Someone who doesn't listen or disregards what you are saying, like NO!

What should you do when someone wants to do more than you want to do and just keeps pressuring you to do more?

7. Avoid dating someone who is not a peer. Someone in a position of power such as your boss, teacher or professor, doctor or counselor, youth leader or pastor may try to use authority to pressure you into sex.

8. Stay sober. A study at a Big Ten university showed that 80 percent of men and 70 percent of women involved in sexual assaults had been drinking.

9. Be assertive. Get angry when someone does something to you that you don't want. Act immediately with some sort of negative response. (You may want to practice this by yourself or with friends.) Stand up for yourself—it's okay to be rude to someone who is sexually pressuring you, even if it hurts his or her feelings. After all, he or she isn't paying attention to your feelings.
10. Know your rights. Any forced sexual contact is illegal. Forced kissing, someone exposing his or her private areas, someone making you touch his or her genitals, someone making you undress, and someone touching your genitals are all considered sexual assault.

    "Rape" is defined as the man's penis penetrating the woman's vagina or a man putting his penis into a boy's or girl's anus. In most states, sex with someone under 16, even if both partners want to do it, is considered "statutory rape" (rape in the legal sense).

What should I do if he forces me to have sex with him?

If one of the above actions occurs, your first decision is whether to report the assault or rape. It's not always an easy decision since you may feel partly responsible. But don't give in to those feelings. What happened, regardless of the circumstances or people involved, wasn't your fault. Remember, no one has a right to force you to have sex.

If you are afraid of what will happen to the offender, especially if that person is a family member or close friend, consider this: If you do not report what was done to you, this person probably will keep assaulting or raping you or other innocent people—maybe even children. Here are some suggestions:

1. Get a medical examination immediately at a hospital emergency room. You can call 911 (or any emergency number) for a ride to the hospital. Even if you're not planning to report the assault or rape to the police, you should get a thorough checkup for the following reasons:

★ First, general body aches result from the tension of rape. A good medical checkup helps you realize that aches and pains are understandable. As well as a general checkup, the doctor will check the area of assault.

★ Second, it's necessary to test for medical problems, venereal disease, or pregnancy.

★ Third, legal evidence is collected. Do not change your clothes or wash before the exam. The doctor will collect the offender's loose pubic hairs. Redness, swelling, scrapes, bumps, bruises, and tenderness will be documented. Clothing worn at the time of the assault also will be examined for evidence.

2. Talk to a trusted adult about your experience. Most states require that your case be reported to the authorities when you tell a teacher, counselor, or pastor about it. It's important for your well-being to be protected from further assault. And you will need emotional and spiritual support in the months to come. Assault and rape are not easy to recover from, but recovery is possible with the proper help (see chapter 26).

Although the questions authorities will no doubt ask may be embarrassing, remember they are trying to build a strong case so the rapist won't hurt anyone else.

If you can't talk to someone you know about it, call one of the nationwide crisis lines. The Rape Abuse Incest National Network (RAINN) at 1-800-656-HOPE will automatically connect you to your local rape crisis center. Or visit my website at www.jameswatkins.com.

Melissa and Brian have been going steady since sixth grade. But now, in eighth grade, they silently sense that they are growing apart. They have increased their physical affection, hoping that by "making love" they can grow closer together again.

Trisha keeps telling David that she loves him, but he

CHAPTER 20

When Will I Know the Right Time for Sex?

never seems convinced. "If you really love me, you'll prove it by making love with me." She really does love him and doesn't want to lose him.

Several guys in gym class keep asking Kyle if he's "made the move" on Aimee. He really doesn't want to. Sometimes he feels like it would be easier, though, to just have sex with Aimee and get the guys off his back.

Aaron took Olivia to Pizza Hut, a movie, and then out for ice cream. On the way to Olivia's house, he pulled off the road and tried to make out with her. When she resisted, Aaron demanded, "Hey, you owe me something for tonight."

What do I do if I really love this guy, but all he wants is sex and doesn't care about me?

Sound familiar? Have you heard similar stories at school? These are just a few examples of ...

Ten Rotten Reasons to Have Sex

1. To "Make" Love

   Melissa and Brian believed that by increasing the physical connection, it would increase their emotional connection. But as we discussed in earlier chapters, intercourse can't *make* love; it can only *express* love. There is no amount of sex—even incredibly good sex—that will create a committed relationship.

   Sex does bind a relationship together, as we mentioned in the last chapter. But without a lifetime commitment, sex becomes less and less meaningful, and the bond begins to splinter. The couple realizes that the only thing holding the relationship together is the feeling that "we've gone too far to turn back now."

   Slowly, but surely, Melissa and Brian began to feel trapped and started to resent each other. No amount of "lovemaking" could make love.

   So if someone is just interested in how far he or she can go with you, go as far as you can go—away!

2. To "Prove" Love

   David is nothing short of a terrorist. He has taken Trisha's emotions hostage and now is making demands. Having sex because we feel forced into it is merely paying ransom, and that's definitely not love.

Why are guys always asking you to "prove" you love them?

Anytime someone asks you to prove your love, you can be sure he or she is only using you. Real love, as we talked about earlier, is patient, not self-seeking, and wants what's best for each person.

Here's what to say if a guy or girl comes on with the if-you-love-me-you'll-prove-it line: "You just proved you don't love me. If you really loved me, you wouldn't make those kinds of demands."

3. To Build Self-Esteem

Remember Show and Tell in elementary school—especially the exhibition after Christmas? Your friends ooh-ed and aah-ed over your official-genuine-super-deluxe toy. You were the envy of the third grade!

Unfortunately, some teens have never outgrown the emotional need for Show and Tell. Their self-esteem isn't based on who they are but on what they wear, whom they date, and who their friends are.

Kyle knows his self-esteem and acceptance by his friends will grow if he brings his official-genuine-super-deluxe Aimee doll to the locker room Show and Tell. (And you can be sure that Aimee's friends keep asking her about her new toy too.)

After you have sex with someone, why does that person dump you like you were a used paper towel?

Unfortunately, after the post-Christmas display, a lot of toys get dumped into the closet, never to be taken out again. The same is true with people. If Concordia Publishing House had a nickel for every person dumped after sex, it could afford to give these books away! Learn to build your self-esteem by rereading chapter 4, not by bragging about your new toy at Show and Tell.

4. To Be Socially Accepted

   Acceptance by your friends is closely related to self-esteem. Right now, as a teen, your friends' opinions mean more than they ever have or ever will again.

But if you think all your friends are "doing it," a Lou Harris poll should change your opinion. The survey discovered that only seven out of 100 12- to 13-year-olds have had sexual intercourse. In the age group of 14 to 15, only one out of four reported having intercourse. In the total survey of 12- to 17-year-olds, only 28 percent have had intercourse!

These statistics reveal two important facts: A lot of Kyle's and Aimee's friends—as well as yours—are lying about their sexual experiences. Roughly three out of four teens have not had intercourse.

Why do people tease you if you're a virgin?

Why is sex becoming such a contest? It's like people think it's cool to lose your virginity at 10 years old!

And peer pressure to have sex is based on those lies. Nearly three-fourths of all girls and half of all guys who have had intercourse felt that they were pressured by society into doing it. One-fourth of girls and guys who have had intercourse said they were personally pre sured to do it by their friends.

But everybody is *not* doing it. So you don't need to feel as though you're some kind of freak if you're a virgin. There are three times more teenage virgins than nonvirgins! So who does that make the real freaks?

5. **To "Pay" for a Date**

As I mentioned in chapter 12, you don't owe anyone your body. It is something you choose to give—with no purse strings attached. And God intended for you to save the gift for your future spouse. So the next time a date demands "payment," try one of these lines:

"Here's ten bucks. Now we're even!"

"You're going to have to take me to more than a movie. You're going to have to take me on a honeymoon."

And, if you're really angry, "What do I look like, a prostitute?"

6. **To Prove Your "Manhood" or "Womanhood"**

Some teens have sex just to see if everything is working. That's like sitting down at a piano when you've never had lesson one and expecting to make beautiful music. The piano has been finely crafted at the factory, so there's no question that the instrument can make beautiful music. (And your body is built better than any Steinway or Baldwin concert grand!)

But the first sexual experiences are almost always awkward and often painful because good sex requires a lot of practice in a secure and stable relationship—one where your partner won't be going away. In other words, within the context of marriage.

How do you know what to do the first time? And how do you know if you're any good at it?

Without the security of marriage, sex becomes stressful: "If I don't do this right, he'll probably not want to see me again." "If I go too early, she won't be satisfied and will think less of me as a man." It's like trying to impress someone at a piano recital when we've never had a lesson or one hour's practice.

But when there's the lifetime commitment of marriage, there's plenty of time to practice. We don't have to feel humiliated if we strike the wrong keys. Before long, we're playing just the right notes. Even after 25 years of marriage, Lois and I are still discovering new ways to make even more beautiful music.

Marriage also eliminates the need to sneak around for piano lessons—and it takes the worry out of somebody catching you practicing!

7. To Gain "Experience"

Let's continue the piano illustration. Every instrument has a different touch or feel to it. An electronic keyboard plays very differently than a concert grand. Okay, they both have 88 keys made of ivory and ebony (or white and black plastic). And they both create musical notes when you strike the keys. But that's where the similarities end.

The same is true of sex. Different people respond differently. One thing may turn one person on, while the same action may be a real turnoff to another person. Each person has different timing as well.

Isn't it good to get some experience before marriage?

So the "experience" you get with Person A may not work with Person B. And even if you're experienced with Persons C through Y, those past experiences probably won't work with Person Z. Talk about a lack of security!

We only bring two kinds of experience into a marriage: no experience or the wrong experience. And the wrong experience is always harder to overcome than no experience.

8. To Get Pregnant

For some girls, pregnancy is a ticket to: A) Force a guy to marry her (which doesn't work most of the time); B) Get out of the house and out on her own, courtesy of the welfare department; C) Hurt or embarrass her parents; D) Prove she's a woman. (This is particularly true in poor areas of the world where having children is the woman's primary "job.") Sadly, these reasons take the wonder and beauty out of sex, don't they?

9. To Feel Good

There's no denying that sex feels incredibly good—but so do drugs. Both, if abused, can cause lifelong heartache or worse. (A quick glance at chapter 22 reveals that casual sex can be as deadly as illegal drugs.)

You're gonna have sex someday, so why not just do it and get it over with?

10. To "Just Do It"

When sex becomes simply recreation or something to do when you're bored, it loses its meaning. If there's one point I want to make about sex, it's this: Sex is too wonderful and beautiful to be abused. Don't use it to prove something. Don't let anyone pressure you into it. And don't use it to satisfy your own physical and emotional needs without thought of your partner's well-being.

Five Great Reasons to Have Sex

Okay, enough "don'ts." Here are five great reasons to have sex!

1. To Express a Lifelong Commitment

Physical affection is only meaningful when an equal amount of commitment is present. (Remember, we talked about this in earlier chapters.) Intercourse was created by God to celebrate a lifelong commitment: "At the beginning the Creator 'made them male and female,' and said, 'For this reason a man will leave his father and mother and be united to his wife, and the two will become one flesh' ... So they are no longer two, but one. Therefore what God has joined together, let man not separate" (Matthew 19:5–6).

I've purposefully listed commitment before love in the list of reasons for sex. That's because feelings of love may not last a lifetime. (Remember, we said that romantic feelings tend to grow weaker after six to 24 months.) But *agape*—the committed kind of love—scan keep growing stronger throughout the marriage.

Total sexual intimacy (intercourse) before a total commitment (marriage), then, creates several problems.

★ It weakens trust between partners. A partner may wonder, If he can't wait for sex until marriage, how can I be sure he will be faithful to me after we're married? In fact, studies show that those who have more than one sexual partner before marriage are more likely to have extramarital affairs. But if you and your partner keep from having intercourse while you're dating and engaged, then you can be reasonably sure that he or she won't be having an affair after you're married.

★ It lessens the importance of sex as a symbol of commitment. How would you feel if you knew several other girls had previously worn your engagement ring? It wouldn't be as special as if you had been the only person to wear it. The same is true with intercourse. If you have or your partner has had sex with just one other person, then intercourse can't be a unique expression of your love.

★ It lessens the commitment itself. For 10 years, Dr. Nancy Moore Clatworthy, sociologist from Ohio State, has been researching couples who have lived together. She's discovered some important reasons to go the whole way to a wedding and marriage license before going all the way.

> First, couples who lived together, then got married, often fantasize about breaking up. Guess how many of those who didn't live together before marriage checked that answer. None! And two out of three "live-in" relationships did not end in marriage—they just ended.
>
> A second question on the survey asked about the couple's "usual level of happiness." One possible answer was "extremely unhappy." The only couples checking that answer were the ones who had lived together.

Want to guess how many of those who didn't live together before marriage checked that answer? None, again!

Third, Dr. Clatworthy's survey asked questions about "finances, household matters, recreation, demonstration of affection, and friends." In every area, the couples who had lived together before marriage disagreed more often than couples who had not.

Dr. Clatworthy also reports, "The finding that surprised me most concerned sex. Couples who had lived together before marriage disagreed about it most often."

The researcher concludes, "For people who are in love, anything less than full commitment is a cop-out. Many girls have found, to their sorrow, that they lost the best partner they might have had by living with him."[14]

Sex and commitment can't be separated. The research shows that total intimacy without total commitment leads to concerns of breaking up, often "extreme unhappiness," and more disagreements—especially about sex.

2. To Express a Lifelong Love

Let me share part of a letter I wrote my daughter when she and my wife had "the talk." I wrote it to her when she was 9, so the language is a bit young, but you'll get the idea.

When you like someone, you like to share with him or her. You share your thoughts: what you like, what's "yucky" or "gross," ideas, stories, jokes, riddles, and things you've learned.

You also like to share your feelings: what's fun, what's scary, what makes you happy, sad, proud, embarrassed, or angry.

You also like to tell that person about your spiritual life: what you think about God, what you pray about, how God is helping you.

That's what friends are for: to share your thoughts, feelings, and spiritual life.

When you really like someone, you also want to share your body. That's why Mom and I like to hug and kiss. And that's why we like to hug and kiss you and Paul. There are also "tickle bug attacks," scratching backs, wrestling, rubbing sore legs, and putting an arm around you when we're talking or watching TV.

For married people, there is also sex. Some other names for it are "making love" or "intercourse." This is a special kind of sharing just for husbands and wives. It says, "I love you more than any other person in the whole world."

Some teens (and adults) think it's fun to have sex with a lot of people. But sex can't be special if you have it with more than one person.

If Mom and I hugged and kissed every boy or girl we saw, hugging and kissing wouldn't be special to you and Paul. Or if Mom kissed a lot of men, it wouldn't be special to me.

And so, sex can only be super special if you save sex for your future husband.

3. To Give and Receive Pleasure

There's no doubt that sex feels good. Take a look at these quotes from literature.

A queen writes: "Kiss me again and again, for your love is sweeter than wine. ... The king lies on his bed, enchanted by the fragrance of my perfume. My beloved one is a sachet of myrrh lying between my breasts."

The king responds: "Oh, how delightful you are; how pleasant, O love, for utter delight! You are tall and slim like a palm tree, and your breasts are like its clusters of dates. I said, I will climb up into the palm tree and take hold of its branches. Now may your breasts be like grape clusters, and the scent of your breath like apples, and your kisses as exciting as the best wine, smooth and sweet."

A wise man gives advice to young men: "Let her charms and tender embrace satisfy you. Let her love alone fill you with delight."

Wow! And guess where these PG-13 quotes are from? The Bible! (Song of Solomon 1:2, 12–13; 7:6–9; and Proverbs 5:19 TLB). God is very much in favor of sexual pleasure. And sex does feel good, whether you're married or not. (Your body doesn't know if you've said, "I do" before you do it.)

But sex that is *just* physical lacks the security of a lifelong commitment. That's why Scripture is also very explicit about no sex until marriage.

Pleasure-only sex lacks another great reason for sex:

4. To Grow Closer Together Mentally, Emotionally, and Spiritually

Becoming "one flesh" also creates one mind, one heart, and one soul.

I know you're not going to believe this next statement. I didn't believe it when I heard it in junior high, either: **Sex is only 10 percent physical.**

I warned you it was unbelievable. But after 25 years of marriage, I'm convinced it's true. Sure, the physical pleasure is just as intense in marriage (actually, it's much, much better!), but there is also a mental, emotional, and spiritual intimacy that often overpowers the physical pleasure.

You still don't believe it, do you? Trust me on this one. When experienced in a loving, married relationship, sex makes partners one in many wonderful ways!

5. To Bring New Life into the World

I've intentionally placed this reason last. That's because I believe that sex was created for many more reasons than just making babies. (Research has shown that God has designed women to be most desirous for sex when they are least likely to become pregnant, so I don't buy some religions' argument that sex is only to be engaged in to produce babies.)

Sex expresses love and commitment, gives pleasure, and bonds partners closer together. But making babies is also a great reason for sex. A loving and stable marriage is the perfect environment to create new life. (Isn't that amazing? We human beings can actually create new life with our bodies!)

So there we have 10 rotten and five great reasons to have sex.

Several teens who filled out our survey asked these typical questions:

Every time I look at a girl, I want to have sex. Am I weird or what?

CHAPTER

21 How Do You Break Habits?

How do you control yourself when things get hot and heavy?

My boyfriend and I are trying to cool the sex, but when I'm at his house and no one else is home, I want it so bad. What can we do?

What do you do if you ask God to help you keep pure and it doesn't help?

I learned the secret to breaking habits in high school journalism class. Mrs. Leiter demanded that every hard news story contain five Ws and an H. It didn't matter if we were covering the football playoffs or the health department's closing of the school pool; we had to tell our readers who, what, where, when, why, and how.

If you're struggling with a habit and nothing—not even prayer—seems to help, ask yourself these questions:

What?

That may sound like a no-brainer. "It's the habit, stupid!" But as the Alcoholics Anonymous program states, knowing that something has become a habit is the "first step." When I realized I had eaten a whole bag of Oreo's in one afternoon, I realized I was powerless over chocolate. (Unfortunately, there's no Chocoholics Anonymous.)

Who?

Is there a particular person or group that you usually do this with?

Jeremy used to limp into my office at least once a week. "I'm so discouraged. I gave in and smoked dope again. I went over to Tim's to see my old friends, and before I knew it, I had a joint in my hand." Jeremy was sincerely interested in helping his friends. But he wasn't strong enough to continue his old relationships without them influencing him.

If every time you're with a particular person, you start cutting down people, smoking, drinking, going too far sexually, or (you fill in the habit), you need to limit your time with that person. Breaking up with old friends is difficult, but your physical or spiritual survival may depend on it.

Where?

Have you noticed that certain locations create different moods—school creates boredom (at least it did for me) or sitting at your desk puts you in a study mood? (That's why you should always do your homework in a special place. After a few weeks, your mind will automatically shift into "study" mode whenever you're at that spot. Studying in bed rarely works because you spend most of your time there sleeeeeeeeping.)

The same principle works for habits. Ray used to sneak down to the basement for a bottle of wine hidden behind the furnace. "It was really weird, Jim. I thought I had beaten my urge to drink. But today, when I was helping my dad change furnace filters, that temptation came back really bad!"

So, if at all possible, stay clear of those locations that tempt you or where you used to engage in that habit. If you find yourself going too far at your "steady's" house when no one else is home, then simply stay away from that tempting location.

If it's a place you absolutely can't avoid such as the bathroom, at least be on your guard. Temptation is going to be particularly strong there! But each time you don't give in there, you begin to break that association with the habit and that location.

When?

Have you noticed that temptations seem greater at certain times? Maybe it's the time of day or when you're tired, worried, depressed, or not feeling well. (I get tempted to eat my body weight in dark chocolate when I'm depressed or bored.)

Obviously you can't change monthly cycles, the time of day, your health, or the phases of the moon. But you can be aware of when temptation seems to be strongest—and be prepared for it. If you know that at 10:00 every night you'll be tempted to clean out the fridge in a feeding frenzy, try calling a friend or being with your parents during that time.

Temptation is ruthless and will attack when you're at your lowest point physically, emotionally, or spiritually.

Why?

Real success begins with the question *why.* Try to discover what need you're trying to satisfy by indulging in the habit. Be honest.

Sheila confessed that she was hooked on sex. She didn't care who the guy was or if she really liked him. Most of her time had been spent hanging around video arcades waiting for someone to pick her up for a "one-nighter."

As we talked, she poured out her unhappy childhood. "I never remember my parents ever hugging me or telling me that they loved me. I craved for someone—anyone—to hold me and tell me they loved me. It didn't matter if they meant it or not. I just wanted to hear it."

Sheila began to feel accepted by the youth group and sensed unconditional love from the teens and the sponsors. The void was now being filled in a positive, safe way.

How?

God wants to help us meet that need. Habits only give us temporary relaxation, security, or release from frustration. But a relationship with God can provide a permanent solution.

He'll probably help you through people in your church or youth group. In 1 Corinthians 10:13, Paul tells us that we are not alone in our temptations. In fact, your youth leader probably struggled with the same habits, drives, or feelings. Talk to him or her. Look to Christian friends for support and prayer. And, as always, turn to your Savior. Paul concludes 1 Corinthians 10:13 by telling us that God will provide a way out of any temptation you face.

You *can* break habits before they break you!

At least two reasons exist for all the talk about "safe sex."

First, 55,000 people get a sexually transmitted disease every day. Some are deadly, such as AIDS. Many others have no cure. (We'll talk about sexually transmitted diseases, or STDs, in the next chapter.)

CHAPTER

22 How Safe Is "Safe" Sex?

Second, more than one million teens get pregnant each year. That's 2,740 each day!

How come everyone is saying to have "safe" sex? Is safe sex really safe?

These are frightening figures. And not knowing the facts about pregnancy, birth control, and STDs is dangerous.

I heard that you can't get pregnant under water. Is that true?

Can you get pregnant if you have sex standing up?

No, having sex under water will not prevent pregnancy. And, yes, you can get pregnant in any position. To answer some other common myths: Yes, you can get pregnant the first time you have sex. No, rhythm birth control has nothing to do with music or moving in rhythm with each other. And, no, rinsing the vagina out doesn't prevent pregnancy.

I'm not sharing this information with you to teach you how to "do wrong the right way." (And for our Catholic readers, I need to remind you that your church takes a strong stand against any "unnatural" form of birth control.) But it's important to let you know that there is no birth control method that is completely, 100 percent effective in preventing pregnancy except abstinence (more on that later).

To help you understand how birth control methods work, let's review the process of conception.

Every 28 days a woman's ovary releases an egg. The egg will be available for fertilization only 12 to 48 hours. The man's sperm cells can live about 24 to 48 hours within the woman's body. This means that during the month a woman can become pregnant for about four days.

If intercourse occurs during this time, 400 million sperm from the male race toward the female's egg. These determined swimmers pass through the cervix into the uterus and up the fallopian tubes where one winner unites with the egg.

From the instant of conception (or fertilization), a new life has begun within the woman. The fertilized egg travels into the uterus where it nestles into the uterine wall, which has been made ready for the egg by becoming thicker with an additional blood supply. If this thickened uterine wall doesn't receive a fertilized egg, it begins to break down and flow from the cervix and vagina as a "period" or menstruation.

Contraceptives work in different ways to keep the sperm from fertilizing the egg. Some forms of birth control keep the fertilized egg from developing to maturity. (Be sure to read chapter 25 if you are considering a birth control method that destroys a developing life.)

The major types of birth control are

Condoms

Condoms (or "rubbers") are very thin tubes of rubber or latex that fit snugly over the man's penis. The semen and sperm are caught in the closed end of the condom, which prevents the sperm from entering the woman's body.

Can condoms get busted or get open somehow while you're having intercourse?

Condoms are not 100 percent effective, however! Failure to prevent pregnancy ranges from 3 to 36 percent. The American Medical Association claims condoms fail in one out of seven incidents. Government tests list the failure rate at 20 percent. This means that condoms don't work up to one-third of the time! A one-in-three chance of becoming pregnant doesn't seem very "safe."

Day-After Pill

By the time you read this book, a morning-after pill may be available in the United States. Most such pills work by causing a miscarriage so the fertilized egg is flushed out of the woman's body at a very early stage of development. It doesn't prevent conception but aborts the growing fetus. So it's basically a do-it-yourself abortion. (Again, check out chapter 25 before you decide that any such method is a good idea.)

Diaphragm

One way to prevent conception is to block the sperm from the entrance to the uterus. A diaphragm is a small, rubber cup with a flexible metal ring. It's placed in the vagina and fits snugly over the cervix (the entrance to the uterus). Spermicide is placed between the diaphragm and the cervix as well as around the outside. (We'll discuss spermicide in a few moments.) The sperm is physically blocked by the barrier and chemically destroyed by the spermicide.

The diaphragm is between 80 and 97 percent effective in preventing pregnancy. This means that you have up to a one-in-five chance of becoming pregnant using this method.

IUD

An IUD, or intrauterine device, is basically a piece of plastic inserted into the uterine wall. A "tail" of plastic thread extends from the uterus, through the cervix, and into the vagina.

No one is quite sure how an IUD works. It's believed that it keeps a fertilized egg from implanting on the uterine wall. Like the day-after pill, it doesn't prevent conception. It causes a fertilized egg to be aborted from the woman's body.

The failure rate is 1 to 6 percent. This means that there is up to a one-in-16 chance of becoming pregnant using this method.

IUDs have been blamed for so many medical problems and have generated such costly lawsuits that this method is rarely used today.

The Pill

Two kinds of oral contraceptives currently exist. The *combination pill* contains two female hormones, which fool the woman's body into thinking it's pregnant. This keeps the woman's egg from being released. Thus, there is no conception.

The *mini-pill* contains only one hormone. Experts believe this pill doesn't prevent the release of eggs but prevents the fertilized egg from implanting on the uterine wall. Again, if you believe that life begins at conception, the mini-pill aborts the new life.

Oral contraceptives are by far the most effective with 99 percent success rate. But they shouldn't be taken by anyone whose family has a history of heart, lung, liver, or kidney diseases, breast or uterine cancer, or migraine headaches.

Norplant

Norplant is a relatively new contraceptive on the market. Six match-sized capsules are surgically inserted below the skin on the inside of a woman's arm, just above her elbow. The hormones, which are slowly released for up to five years, are 99 percent effective in preventing ovulation. Norplant is less effective in women weighing more than 150 pounds.

Side effects in some women include irregular menstrual cycles, nausea, mood changes, occasional headaches, and increase in acne. The implants can be removed by a doctor at any time, and the woman can become pregnant soon after they're removed.

Can you get a girl pregnant if you have sex right before or after a girl's period?

Rhythm

As we mentioned, a woman can only become pregnant during about four days out of the month (usually 10 to 12 days before or after her period). The rhythm method depends on not having sex during those four fertile days. Since a woman can't always tell when she's ovulating, the method is only successful one-half to three-fourths of the time.

Spermicide

Spermicide blocks conception in two ways. First, when the cream, jelly, or foam is inserted in the woman's vagina, it blocks the path to the cervix. Second, the spermicide also kills the man's sperm cells. With this method, the woman has a one-in-four chance of becoming pregnant.

The Sponge

The sponge was reintroduced to the market in late 1999 after being taken off the shelves in 1995 because of bacterial contamination. The new manufacturer claims the over-the-counter device is now 100 percent safe.

The circular piece of polyurethane is treated with spermicide and, when inserted into the vagina, blocks the entrance to the cervix as well as killing sperm. Dr. Robert Hatcher, author of *Contraceptive Technology,* claims it's 91 percent effective when used properly.

Does the pill keep you from getting sexual diseases?

Pregnancy isn't the only consideration. No birth control method is completely effective in preventing sexually transmitted diseases.

Condoms have been advertised as protection against AIDS. However, the *New England Journal of Medicine* reports that condoms are less than 70 percent effective in preventing AIDS or other STDs. That means a person has roughly a one-in-three chance of getting AIDS, even if he or she is using "protection."

Very little research is currently being done on condoms and AIDS because a multimillion dollar grant to the University of California was cut off by the federal government because "condoms may be incapable of providing protection to study participants."[15]

The pill doesn't prevent STDs, either. In fact it increases by two to three times the chances of contracting chlamydia. (We'll discuss this STD in the next chapter.)

Some spermicides are advertised as preventing STDs, but again they are not 100 percent effective.

Let's try to visualize the odds with a game of Russian roulette. In this game—which I'm *not* recommending—the player puts one bullet in a revolver, spins the chamber, puts the barrel to his or her head, and pulls the trigger. If the chamber can hold six bullets, the player has a one-in-six chance of never playing the game again!

Let's pretend you have a 100-chamber "gun." With each of the birth control methods, you put the following number of bullets in the gun:

Method	Bullets
Condoms	20–36
Day-After Pill	NA
Diaphragm	3–20
IUD	1–6
Norplant	1
The Pill	6–18 (for teens!)
Rhythm	25–50
Spermicide	25
Sponge	10
No Birth Control	90

If you knew that 20 to 36 bullets were in the gun, would you pull the trigger? That's how "safe" condoms make sex! Would you pull the trigger with 90 bullets in the gun? Those are the kind of odds you're up against with no protection!

But there's one set of odds I didn't mention:

NO SEX   0

Those are the only odds I'd be willing to play Russian roulette with. How about you?

Christy's boyfriend, Bret, assured her that he had never done drugs or had homosexual sex, so there was no chance of getting AIDS. However, one of Bret's former girlfriends had a partner who did intravenous drugs. Now Christy has HIV.

When you have sexual intercourse, it's like having sex with everyone your partner has had sex with.

CHAPTER

23 How Can You Keep from Getting an STD?

Although Christy only had sex with Bret, she contracted HIV from an unknown partner of Bret's former girlfriend.

The Minnesota Health Department has identified nearly 40 diseases that are spread through all kinds of sexual contact. The U.S. Centers for Disease Control claim the number of sexually transmitted "organisms and syndromes" tops 50! Currently, more than 12 million Americans between the ages of 15 and 55 catch an STD each year with a total of 56 million currently living with incurable STDs. That's one in five in that age group! And that number will probably continue to grow.

Here are the six most prevalent STDs today.

AIDS

Acquired Immune Deficiency Syndrome begins with the human immunodeficiency virus (HIV), which destroys the victim's ability to fight off diseases and infections. Since the victim's body has no defense against it, AIDS is 100 percent deadly. Most victims lose a lot of weight and often die of pneumonia. But AIDS carriers can have no symptoms. (Book two in this series, *Is There Really Life after Death?*, deals at length with AIDS.)

The AIDS virus is spread by blood-to-blood or by semen-to-blood contact through homosexual acts, intercourse, or using dirty hypodermic needles. There is no proof that AIDS can be spread by casual contact (holding hands, hugging, or closed-mouth kissing), since the virus dies very quickly when exposed to air.

When AIDS was first observed, 73 percent of its victims were homosexual men and 17 percent were addicts who shared dirty needles to shoot drugs. Now, 89 percent of AIDS is spread through sexual intercourse between men and women! In America, the fastest growing group of victims is heterosexual teens and young adults. Since the virus can take up to 10 years to show itself, this means that many contracted AIDS in junior high!

The predictions as to how many people have AIDS and how many will die keep changing. Some claim that 250,000 people in America have died already of AIDS. There may be as many as 50 to 100 million carriers of this deadly virus throughout the world. Most carriers don't even realize they have the disease.

Chlamydia

This bacteria is caught by touching the infected part of the person who has it. The bacteria can invade a partner's body through the vagina, urethra, rectum, eyes, or mouth. Since the bacteria can only live in warm, moist places of the body, it quickly dies when outside the body. There is no danger of catching this or any other STD from toilet seats or things the person has touched. You can only catch it by open-mouthed kissing and any kind of sexual contact.

Symptoms of the disease include painful urination and cloudy urine. Women may secrete a cloudy liquid from the vagina. Often there are no symptoms until the reproductive organs have already been damaged.

Chlamydia, if discovered, can be treated with antibiotics. If not treated, it can keep one-fourth of men and women from having children. Also this STD can cause problems in pregnancy such as premature birth or stillbirths. One out of three babies born to carriers will have chlamydia. Of these, 13 percent will have serious birth defects such as blindness, eye infections, and pneumonia.

Each year, 3 to 10 million Americans catch this bacteria. One out of 10 college students has the bacteria. Women taking birth control pills are two to three times more likely to catch chlamydia.

Gonorrhea

This STD, often called "the clap," is caught only by sexual contact. It usually lives in a man's penis and urethra or a woman's cervix. Its symptoms are the same as those for chlamydia.

Most cases can be cured with penicillin or antibiotics. But some men, and most women, don't even realize they have it until it damages their reproductive organs. It also can attack the skin, bones, joints, tendons, and other organs. Two million Americans are infected with gonorrhea each year.

Herpes

Several kinds of herpes virus are known. Herpes simplex virus 1 (HSV-1) causes cold sores or fever blisters and chicken pox.

Herpes simplex virus 2 (HSV-2) is the sexually transmitted form of the disease that affects the sexual organs as well as the lower body. HSV-2 spreads through intercourse, kissing, and touching affected sores. Half of the babies who get HSV-2 from their infected mothers will die; one-fourth will be brain-damaged. An estimated 5 to 30 million Americans now have this STD. Another half million are added to that total each year.

So far, there is no known cure.

Syphilis

This STD lives in the warm, moist areas of the mouth, vagina, and urethra. After sexual contact (kissing or contact with sexual organs), a small red, painless sore appears. These chancres (pronounced "shankers") appear on the penis or on the mouth. They may be present in the vagina or cervix of the woman but not noticeable. In one to five weeks the chancres usually disappear.

But the disease spreads through the blood stream. About six weeks after the sores disappear, the person with syphilis may have a headache, a fever, loss of appetite, and a red skin rash that doesn't itch. Again, these symptoms disappear by themselves. If untreated, all symptoms disappear in about six months.

But the disease silently spreads and years later can cause blindness, heart disease, paralysis, brain damage, or death. Babies born to infected mothers face birth defects or death.

Nearly 100,000 people contract syphilis in the United States each year.

Venereal Warts (or HPV)

Venereal warts or human papillomavirus (HPV) is the number one cause of cervical cancer in women, which in turn kills more than 7,000 women each year. Babies of infected mothers can develop venereal warts in their throats and lungs, which sometimes causes death. One million new victims in the United States are stricken each year with this STD.

How do you avoid these diseases? The only sure way is to remain a virgin, then marry a virgin, then both stay sexually faithful to each other.

As we discovered in the last chapter, no birth control is completely effective in preventing pregnancy. And no birth control comes with a 100 percent guarantee to prevent STDs. The only guarantee for "safe sex" is to "just say no" to sexual contact outside of a faithful marriage relationship.

"I need to talk to you," she usually says without making eye contact. After sitting in the office, her eyes remain downcast as she picks imaginary lint from her sweater.

"So how can I help you?"

There's usually a long silence.

CHAPTER 24

What Do You Say to a Pregnant Friend?

"Well, you know I've been seeing this guy. And … ah … we think we love each other … and …"

She stares at the floor, then her shoulders begin to quiver as the tears begin to form in her eyes.

"I think I'm pregnant," she finally sobs.

So how do you as a friend (or as a youth leader) respond to this situation?

Shockproof

First and foremost, don't show shock.

After more than 20 years of working with young people, I've gotten to the point where not even an eyebrow twitches when I'm told, "I think I'm pregnant,"

"My best friend has AIDS," or "You're pretty cool for being so old." The poker face doesn't mean I don't care, but that I'm a safe person with whom to share one's most shocking secrets.

Often teens will "bait" us with a test question such as "What do you think about abortion?" before asking the real question. If we remain calm and compassionate in answering the trial question, the real issue probably will be brought up.

Once the shock wave subsides, ask, "Are you sure you're pregnant?" If she only suspects she's pregnant, urge her to find out if she really is. Suggest one of the over-the-counter test kits or a visit to a Crisis Pregnancy Center. Having worked with a CPC, I am very impressed with the professional and compassionate manner with which the staff of Christian counselors truly ministers to young women. They can be a terrific source. See my website (www.jameswatkins.com) or your nearest CPC.

At this point, it is important to let her know that you have an idea of what she's feeling. (I've learned that I can never "understand completely" what anyone is feeling—especially since I'm a male and half the population is the opposite gender.) Try something like, "If you're like most young women, you're probably really scared" to open up the discussion. Fear is often her overwhelming emotion: fear of what her boyfriend is going to think and do; fear of how her parents and the church community will react; fear that every dream and goal she's ever worked for will be destroyed. And she's usually afraid of the actual pregnancy.

Use the first meeting to talk about these issues. Assure her that she has your support and prayers. This is not the time to talk about the behavior that led to suspecting pregnancy. (That will come later.) Before she leaves, set up a time a few days later for her to get back with you on the results.

Sharing the Shock

If the tests come back that she is pregnant, her first response probably will be

denial. "The test was wrong!" "This isn't happening to me." Don't let her deny it by refusing to get medical care or by trying to wear tight underclothes to hide the condition. Her health—and the baby's—are crucial.

Other possible reactions are generalized anger (at herself, at her partner, at God, or perhaps even at you as a friend), bargaining ("God, if You make me un-pregnant, I'll never have sex again till marriage, I'll be a missionary, I'll ...), and depression.

If she isn't pregnant, her sexual activity is still a serious problem she needs to deal with. This may be the time to talk about the emotional and spiritual consequences of sex outside of marriage. Whether she is or isn't pregnant, offer her a chance to repent, receive God's forgiveness, then commit to future sexual purity.

If she is pregnant, she may plead, "Don't tell my parents!" I've tried to be careful not to promise complete confidentiality when talking with teens. I always say, "You know I'll keep whatever we say just between us—unless it involves your or someone else's health and safety." This allows freedom to intervene in life-threatening situations, including physical or sexual abuse, drug use, suicidal tendencies, or pregnancies.

Stress that her parents need to know and that they probably will be much more supportive than the girl imagines they will be. Offer to go with her when she tells her parents. Also stress the importance of informing school officials. The school nurse will know school policies and what help is available.

Telling the church is also an important step. I have been pleased with how well our church has responded to young women who have become pregnant. In the most recent situation, several women from the congregation gathered around the girl with hugs and tears after she made her situation public. It has also helped to discuss, in our youth group, how we can support the girl with our prayers and acts of kindness. And at the same time stress the importance of sexual purity.

Sharing the Load

Aside from the emotional issues, there are also some very tangible challenges.

Crisis Pregnancy Centers can help by offering maternity clothing and support groups of other teenage mothers-to-be. A church next door to our local high school offers the "Teen-Parent Co-Op" that offers childcare during school hours so young moms can stay in school.

The courts and welfare department also can make sure that the father of the child takes financial responsibility for the child. (Guys, you're responsible for your sexual behavior—and that includes child support until that "good time" is 18 years old.)

Finally, keep loving her. If she makes an unwise choice such as refusing to admit she's pregnant, aborting the baby, or leaving the church, continue to love her. More than anything else, she needs to know you care and support her. Even if you don't agree with her actions (and you can carefully let her know that), reassure her that you still care and want to help in any way you can.

Beth comes from a good Christian family. Her dad is on the church board, and she's an officer in the youth group. She's an excellent student and has a scholarship to a Christian college. And she just found out she's pregnant.

Here's the letter I sent to Beth after she wrote about her pregnancy. Please consider it as a personal letter to you if you just found out you're pregnant or if a friend just found out she's pregnant.

CHAPTER 25

Isn't an Abortion an Easy Out?

My friend is 14, and she's pregnant. What should she do?

Dear Friend,

Thanks for trusting me by sharing your situation. If you're like most pregnant teens I've talked with, fear is the overwhelming emotion you're feeling. You're afraid of what your parents are going to think of you. You're afraid of what the church will think of you and what the members will think of Mom and Dad. You're afraid that every dream and goal you have ever worked for will be destroyed. You're afraid your boyfriend will desert you. And you're probably afraid of the actual pregnancy.

Abortion seems like the easy way out. At least that's what friends or Planned Parenthood may have told you: "All of your fears can be neatly done away with by a secret trip to our clinic."

But before you consider this "easy way out," please consider these thoughts:

1. Don't limit your options. Your choices are not limited to either keeping the child or aborting the baby. Adoption is a very positive alternative to being a teenage parent. It will probably be difficult to give up your baby. But there are hundreds of couples who yearn to give your baby the love and care he or she deserves.

2. Consider your baby. By the time your fears of pregnancy are confirmed, your baby is already quite developed. His or her heart is beating vigorously. Bones are formed. Fingers, toes, eyes, and ears are clearly defined. He or she has reflexes and can feel pain. By six weeks, his or her skeleton is complete. At seven weeks, brain waves can be registered on an EEG. At eight weeks, his or her stomach, liver, kidneys, and brain are working. After 10 weeks, the only changes that occur are growth in size.

   This is not just a "glob of tissue." It is not even your body. He or she has a separate circulatory system and may even have a different blood type. Very simply, abortion painfully takes the life of a separate and unique human being. You and your unborn child walk into an abortion clinic together. You walk out alone.

Is there any danger in getting an abortion? I hear it's really safe.

3. Consider yourself and your future. Regardless of what Planned Parenthood or others may tell you, an abortion is far more complicated than having your tonsils out. Here are some of the risks:

- ★ One out of three women having abortions develops pelvic inflammatory disease. Those who get this infection often aren't able to have another child.[16]
- ★ After having an abortion, you double your chances of having serious problems with the next pregnancy. One such problem is a pregnancy outside the womb. This threatens the lives of 35,000 women each year. [17]
- ★ Your chances for miscarrying double if you abort your first pregnancy and triple after two or more abortions. (Miscarrying is the death of a baby early in his or her development.) [18]
- ★ The chance of having a premature baby or one with dangerously low birth weight also increases by two to four times after having an abortion. [19]
- ★ You double your chances of getting breast cancer if you abort your first baby during the first three months. [20]
- ★ Between 3 and 5 percent of women who had their first pregnancy aborted will never be able to have another child. [21]
- ★ One out of 20 women have their cervix damaged during an abortion. This is the muscle that seals off the uterus from the vagina. Injuries to the cervix can lead to heavy bleeding, miscarriage, and premature births in future pregnancies. [22]
- ★ One out of 50 women having abortions will need a blood transfusion because of massive internal bleeding. This is usually caused by the abortionist accidentally puncturing the uterine wall. [23]

Besides these physical dangers, the psychological and emotional scars cannot be ignored. The British Medical Journal reports that "almost all those [who have abortions] feel guilt and depression" for at least a brief period of time.[24] The British Journal of Obstetrics and Gynecology claims that "guilt feelings, nervous symptoms, sleeplessness, and feelings of regret" last up to eight weeks.[25] But The Archives of Psychological Research reports that "the young women in our study have only a 50 percent chance of getting over the abortion experience within five to seven months."[26]

Dr. Anne Speckhard of the University of Minnesota has cataloged these effects that occurred five to 10 years after an abortion:

- ★ Eighty-one percent reported preoccupation with the aborted child.
- ★ Nearly three out of four reported flashbacks of the actual operation.
- ★ Fifty-four percent recalled nightmares about the abortion.
- ★ Over one-third had visions of the aborted child visiting them.
- ★ And nearly one out of four reported hallucinations related to the abortion.[27]

No wonder that in a five-year study researchers discovered that one out of four women who had had abortions was under psychiatric care. (That's eight times the number of women getting psychiatric help who didn't have abortions.)

I don't mean to scare you. But you need to ask yourself, am I willing to risk these physical and emotional scars for the rest of my life?

I think I'm pregnant, but I just can't tell my parents. What should I do?

4. Don't cut your parents out of your decision. Abortion clinics take

advantage of your fears, especially the fear that your parents will find out. But many girls discover that their parents turn out to be the strongest and most understanding support during this time.

My friend Gay Lewis has written an excellent book called *Bittersweet*. She writes about how she and her daughter, who was unmarried and pregnant, grew closer together through this difficult time.

It won't be easy to tell your parents. Gay's daughter wrote a letter. And Mom and Dad probably won't have easy answers. But they are probably in the best position to give you the loving support you need to do the right thing.

5. Seek out your nearest Crisis Pregnancy Center. It's probably listed in the phone book. If not, call the nearest Right to Life group. These centers are staffed by caring, committed volunteers. They can offer counseling, as well as referrals for medical services and even housing, if needed.

6. Don't throw out your spiritual life. God won't desert you. Forgiveness for sin, even sexual sin, is still available. You need no more forgiveness because you've been "caught" than if you hadn't.

   Obviously, asking God to forgive you will not erase your pregnancy, but it will restore your relationship with Him. And you'll receive His strength and assurance of His forgiveness as you face the days ahead. His strength will help you make the right decisions for yourself and the unborn child within you.

With you in this crisis,

Jim

"My friend Kathy needs to talk to you," Heather almost whispered as she slipped into my office with a friend in tow. "Well, gotta go." With that, the youth group's president disappeared, leaving Kathy looking frightened and alone.

"Hi, Kathy," I began. "Would you like to have a seat?"

CHAPTER

26 Can You Become a Virgin Again?

The girl, who looked about 15, quickly sat down and stared at the floor. "So," I began, trying to break the icy silence, "How do you know Heather?"

"From school," she said quietly, still staring at the floor.

"Do you have some classes together?"

"Yeah."

After a few minutes of trying to keep the conversation going, I finally asked, "Would you like to tell me why you're here?"

Her body began to shake, then the tears began to stream.

"My father ... he ... he ..." The words seemed to catch in her throat.

"Did your father abuse you, Kathy?"

She nodded.

"Did he sexually abuse you?"

"Yes," she nearly screamed. "He and my two brothers!"

My dad forced me to do a lot of weird things when I was little—not really intercourse—but a lot of feeling around. Now I feel really used.

After a few moments she composed herself and began to tell me the story. After seven years of abuse, Kathy had gone to her school counselor. Now she was in a Christian foster home where she had come to know Jesus as her Savior. Although Christ does make us "new creations" instantly, it often takes months or years for us to view ourselves as brand-new.

As we talked almost weekly for the next six months, I discovered a girl who felt betrayed, abandoned, alone, unable to trust any kind of authority, confused about self-identity, violated, disrespected, used, dirty, trapped, robbed, guilty, responsible for the acts, full of love-hate feelings toward her family, and depressed.

To help her understand what had happened, we talked about how

A Sexual Relationship Dramatically Changes a Person

It's not simply something you "do." It's not just "getting physical." It's an act that changes a person emotionally, socially, mentally, and physically.

I had sex with a guy when I was 12. I realize now it was dumb, but how do I deal with it?

The first time I had sex it was awful. Is there something wrong with me?

The first experience is usually less than successful and satisfying. If outside the security of marriage, it can create a negative view of sex. Often the disappointment destroys the relationship premarital sex promised to develop.

An 18-year-old writes:

> Sex is 99 percent mental fulfillment. It will be wonderful when it is clean, guilt-free, done from love, and with God's blessing. [My experience with premarital sex] was cold, embarrassing, lonely, and dangerous.

Another teen wrote:

> We felt totally empty afterward, and feelings of hate and distrust came between us. I wondered how many other girls he had slept with, and he wondered how many other guys I had yielded to.

These reactions, emotions, and fears (especially in cases of rape and incest) can damage our healthy, God-given attitudes toward sex in marriage.

My girlfriend and I had oral sex, but we really haven't had intercourse. Are we still virgins?

What about the couples who may still be virgins technically (there's been no vaginal penetration) but have been involved in heavy petting and oral sex? Author Walter Trobisch claims there are still drastic changes.

> Virginity is not just a mark of the body. To me it is much more a question of the heart, or the ability to love. It is not something someone loses, but something they give.
>
> Everyone has a unique gift—the ability to give himself or herself completely to only one. This gift is like [money] in the bank. But many spend it in small coins. Every day they draw a little out of their [bank account] and in flirtation, here and there, throw it to the wind. Technically speaking, they may still be virgins, but they have lost their ability to love through a lot of necking and petting experiences.[28]

In other words, a couple may be virgins on a technicality since there was no vaginal penetration. But they have given so much of their bodies to each other, that they are no longer virgins mentally, emotionally, and spiritually. (Remember, I said that sex was only 10 percent physical.) And sometimes losing one's mental virginity is more harmful emotionally than losing it physically.

But there is hope!

Once you've lost your virginity, can you ever get it back?

A Relationship with God Dramatically Changes a Person

As I mentioned in chapter 16, the church in Corinth was filled with Christians who had been involved in all kinds of immoral behavior before they believed in Christ. The apostle Paul lists "those who live immoral lives, ... who are adulterers or homosexuals" (1 Corinthians 6:9–10 TLB).

He goes on to say, "There was a time when some of you were just like that but now your sins are washed away, and you are set apart for God, and He has accepted you because of what the Lord Jesus Christ and the Spirit of our God have done for you" (verse 11 TLB).

Perhaps you're bound by other vices: pornography, lustful thoughts, jealousy, or (you fill in the blank). Jesus' promise of freedom (see John 8:32) applies to every kind of bondage.

Can God really forgive me for what I've done?

A Relationship with God Makes a Person Brand-New

In John 3:16, Jesus declares that "whoever believes in Him" starts life over! Regardless of our past and behavior, we are innocent in God's eyes.

Paul also writes, "When someone becomes a Christian he becomes a brand new person inside. He is not the same any more. A new life has begun!" (2 Corinthians 5:17 TLB). Unfortunately, we can't deliberately forget the way God can. But He has provided a way that we can experience mental healing as well.

A Relationship with God Makes a Person's Mind Brand-New

As Kathy and I talked over the next few months, she began to see herself as this "brand-new person." One week she shared two Scripture passages that had been helpful to her.

> Don't copy the behavior and customs of this world, but be a new and different person with a fresh newness in all you do and think. (Romans 12:2 TLB)
>
> Now your attitudes and thoughts must all be constantly changing for the better. Yes, you must be a new and different person, holy and good. Clothe yourself with this new nature. (Ephesians 4:23-24 TLB)

Kathy's freedom from her past wasn't, however, easy.

A Relationship with God Doesn't Change Everything

Unfortunately, some things do not change because we ask forgiveness for our past and become members of God's family. Social and natural consequences do not change. Innocence in God's eyes—and our own—doesn't change our earthly reputation. But don't let that keep you from changing! The good news will get around; it just travels slower than bad news.

Sexually transmitted diseases or pregnancy are not taken care of with a quick prayer, either. Medical and emotional treatment may be necessary. Some legal obligations may need to be fulfilled. For instance, a guy may be paying child support for the next 18 years for one night's actions.

The worst part of being abused is the vivid memories. How do I deal with all that stuff?

Memories don't change at salvation, either. We can never completely forget our past, but the memories will fade and no longer control us as God "renews our minds."

There's one last area that won't change: other people. People don't change—at least not without God's help. They may promise to change their behavior toward you, but only God can cause a person to be "reborn." If you're in a situation where you are being physically or sexually abused, your first responsibility is to get out of that relationship. Now!

Your pastor or school counselor can put you in touch with juvenile authorities who will give you protection. They can get help for those who are hurting you as well. You can't change the situation by yourself, and you're not helping anyone by protecting an abuser. And while the person hurting you may not turn to God and repent of his or her actions, God can give you the power and freedom to love and forgive your abuser. And He can give you love and forgiveness for yourself.

It has taken a lot of time, prayer, and professional counseling, but today Kathy has learned to cope with her past. She's learned to forgive her father and brothers and is now happily married. God can do the same for you and your friends.

CAN YOU BECOME A VIRGIN AGAIN?

Part FIVE

Can You Die from Puberty?

The word *puberty* sounds so sinister. You can almost imagine a doctor coming into the examining room with that you-have-six-months-to-live look on his face.

"I'm sorry," he says, grasping one of your hands with both of his. "But I'm afraid the tests have all

CHAPTER

27 A Final Note

come back positive. You have ... puberty."

Let me assure you, no one has ever died of adolescence! In fact, this stage of life is anything but terminal—it's *very* temporary! Your acne will clear up, you will stop outgrowing your clothes and tripping over your own feet, you will get along with your parents once more, your emotions will become stable again, and chances are good you will meet Mr. or Ms. Right.

I hope this book has assured you these changes are normal, healthy, and temporary and whatever your stage of development, *you* are normal and healthy.

I also hope you have sensed the importance of finding answers to your questions from reliable sources such as parents, teachers, youth leaders, and pastors. And I trust you've realized that the God who created your body, mind, and spirit has the changeless answers for the confusing questions in your life.

Last of all, I hope we'll have the chance to meet face-to-face sometime at a youth camp or conference. Until then, drop me a note at whyfiles@jameswatkins.com or in care of the publisher. Or stop by my website at www.jameswatkins.com.

Dear friend,

I pray that you may enjoy good health and that all may go well with you, even as your soul is getting along well.

(3 John 2)

Jim

Appendix A

A Special Message to Parents

Before public schools taught sex education, my friend Chuck was conducting his own "classes" at the back of the bus. His curriculum consisted of magazines he had found stashed in his dad's workshop. One day he announced with great authority, "Rhythm birth control is having sex while listening to the radio." (Do not try this at home!)

Another educational tool I found fascinating was the *Family Medical Book* my aunt and uncle kept on a high shelf in the closet. For 25 cents, my cousin would sneak it into his room for a peek at chapters 17 and 18. (I think he finally bought a mountain bike with the money he collected from friends.)

Unfortunately, most sex education occurs at the back of the bus, at a cousin's house, in the locker room, and wherever kids meet—and much of it is misinformation. Where would our kids really like to find out about sex? Parents! Yep, that's what the Search Institute has learned, but only one in 14 parents discusses sex with his or her children.

Like many parents, you may feel awkward about bringing up the subject with your children. But let's face it—it's us or the bus! Lois and I vowed that our children would hear about the beauty and wonder of sexuality before some second-grade Masters and Johnson told them!

The ideal would be to begin sex education at the moment of birth. Hugging, kissing, and warmth of human contact show a child the beauty of communicating love with our bodies. Parents can use teachable moments such as children discovering their body parts, Mom being pregnant with a younger sibling,

Mom nursing a new baby, discovering tampons on the top shelf of the closet (one mother told her son they were cigars!), or bringing home a new word (with four letters, of course). You don't have to worry about bringing up the subject with small children! But you may have avoided the topic by saying, "Someday we'll have the talk." So now that "someday" is here, how can we openly talk about the subject?

Answer the Questions They're Asking

If they ask about "A," don't give them "A–Z." We've tried to keep a bit ahead of what our children—and their peers—already knew. If kids were talking about "M" on the playground, we made sure we were talking about "N–P" at home.

Plan Some "Big" Events

When Faith was in fourth grade, Lois took her to the local Holiday Inn for a weekend of swimming, miniature golf, and eating pizza on the king-size bed. During this time, Lois explained the wonderful—and normal—changes Faith should expect in the next few years. Since I wanted to get in on the educational process, I wrote a letter to my favorite 9-year-old, to use when Lois got to the part about the sperm and egg getting together. (See chapter 15.)

My trip to the Holidome with Paul came in second grade. We discovered he was hearing about "N" already and we had just talked about "O," so we accelerated his education.

In our teaching we've avoided the concept of "good" and "bad" touches that is often taught in schools. Because we don't want Faith and Paul to think that sex is "bad," we've used the terms "family and friend" touches and "husband and wife" touches. We don't want them to be emotionally confused when suddenly "bad" touches become "good" touches after they say, "I do."

So we've tried not to teach anything we'll need to un-teach, such as babies coming from cabbage patches, the Tooth Fairy transforming bicuspids into coins, and "Grandpa is just sleeping."

Allow the Subject to Come Up Naturally

Hug and kiss a lot! (Put this book down right now and give your spouse a big, wet kiss!) Let your children know that physical affection is designed to express joy and love in close relationships. Let me warn you, however, that knowledge is dangerous in a grade-schooler's brain! And we have tried to teach them that what they're learning is not for school's Show and Tell or for family reunions.

Once, Lois was in the shower after spending several hours weeding strawberries. As the stream of water massaged her sore, aching muscles, she was murmuring, "Ooooo. Aaaah. Oh, yeah!" Paul knocked on the door and yelled, "Are you and Dad having sex in there?!" Another time, when Paul was 3 and visiting my parents, he suddenly announced, "Grandpa, I have a penis! Do you have a penis?" My father turned bright red and just stared into his mashed potatoes. Which brings us to another point.

Remain Cool and Calm

My father turned bright red another time. As a sixth-grader I wrote in the dust of our 1965 Chevy, "Make love, not war." Dad went ballistic and growled, "Wash that off right now and never, ever say 'make love' again!" I just thought it meant it was better to love people than bomb them. I found out differently at the back of the bus. And I also discovered that sex was an unspeakable subject with Dad.

That's why it's so important that we parents maintain a calm, matter-of-fact expression when our kids ask, "What's a condom?" or "How do you get AIDS?" Admittedly it takes some practice to react calmly to, "Where can a person get an early pregnancy test?" (See chapter 24 for the answer to that one.)

If we have a history of being cool and calm when the subject comes up, the subject will keep coming up.

Be Accurate

Even good communication can be broken off with bad information. When I was in third grade, my mom told me that a baby lived inside a mother's stomach. This poor, ignorant woman, I thought. According to my science book, a baby would have to survive hydrochloric acid in the stomach, then have to squeeze through several feet of intestines to get out. Yeccchhhh! I knew that couldn't happen, so I stopped asking Mom questions and started asking Chuck instead.

Keep Lines of Communication Open

Most of all, deliberately work at ways to get beyond the "What did you do in school today?" "Nothing" dialogue.

1. Do things with your teen. Take your son or daughter out to eat—just Mom and son or Dad and daughter. Do things that allow you to spend lengthy amounts of time together.

   People look at me like I'm some kind of sexual deviant as I sit outside of women's dressing rooms (which always seem to be in the bra and panty section), but Faith loves to shop and I love to be with her. Once a week, Paul and I try to have "Men's Night" where we build something or just watch TV, drink Pepsi, and see who can belch the loudest.
2. Look through the books they bring home from school. Ask, "What do you think about ...?" (Remember, keep questions nonthreatening.)
3. Watch TV with them.
4. Talk about TV commercials. "Do you think using (fill in the blank) will really make you (fill in the blank)?"
5. Talk about why you don't allow certain TV programs in your home.
6. Talk about the TV news. (Every night there's an opportunity to talk about everything from AIDS to zygote cryogenics.)

7. Talk about music. Ask, "What do you think about that singer's attitude toward women?" "Why do you think that singer has such a bad attitude toward men?"
8. Talk about the message presented at your house of worship last weekend.
9. Play communication games, such as the Ungame. This board game allows for nonthreatening communication of real feelings.
10. Talk about what you're feeling. (Don't make your kids take the first step.)

Sometimes it's as difficult as getting a "childproof" cap off a bottle, but keep trying. Your children do want to hear about sex from you—not at the back of the bus.

APPENDIX B

A Special Message to Teachers and Youth Leaders

As you read the previous message to parents, you may have asked, "How can I help parents teach their children about sexuality?" Here is a plan that has worked for many organizations and churches.

Get Approval for Parents' Meetings

As a just-out-of-college youth worker, the first thing I learned was boards do not like surprises!

1. Send a letter to all parents of children from 5 to 15. Begin by documenting the need. My survey of 1,000 junior highers (see the introduction) should convince parents that children and teens are looking for answers.

   Ask if they would be interested in a series of meetings that would help them teach their values and beliefs to their children. Then call them. (I got a better response to phone calls than to response slips.)

   Once you're convinced the parents are eager for it, you're ready for step two. (If you skip step one, the board will view this as "your program," and it will probably die in committee. But if the majority of parents express a desire for it, it will probably be approved.)

2. Prepare course objectives, as well as a list of resources such as books, films, and guest speakers. I've used the following:

Objectives: To equip parents to teach their children ...

★ sound medical information on sexual development at appropriate age levels.

★ moral principles relating to sexual behavior at appropriate age levels.

★ a healthy appreciation for their sexual makeup and ways to assist them to make wise choices in sexual behavior.

Resources:

Concordia Publishing House is a leader in home-based sex education that covers all the bases (pun intended) from preschoolers through young adults. How to Talk Confidently with Your Child about Sex is also available, plus a great resource for adults called **Human Sexuality**. Visit the Concordia Publishing House web site at www.cphmall.com.

Teen-Aid provides a complete sex education program for junior high and high schools. The curriculum is based on Judeo-Christian values but is written and designed for public or private schools. (Teen-Aid, Inc., N. 1330 Calispel, Spokane, WA 99201)

True Love Waits from the Southern Baptists provides tapes, videos, and printed material that is very contemporary.

Josh McDowell's **Why Wait** campaign includes books and videos to help your children say no to sexual pressure. *How To Help Your Child Say 'No' to Sexual Pressure* is excellent. (Josh McDowell Ministries, Box 1000, Dallas, TX 75221)

Your local Youth for Christ or Young Life director would welcome the opportunity to share with parents and teens.

3. Go to the board prepared with responses from parents, along with course objectives, resources, and staff suggestions. You'll also want to be prepared for these possible objections:

★ "The schools are already teaching sex education." Many schools are merely teaching the physics of sexuality without providing any kind of moral values. Worse, some schools are teaching values that are contrary to those of many parents and most churches.

★ "We never had it when I was a kid, and I turned out okay." One teen camp at which I spoke was held at the same time as the district's family camp. At every service there were more than 50 people who were 50 years old sitting on the back benches. After speaking about masturbation one morning, a little old lady with her hair in a bun came hobbling down the aisle. "Brother Watkins," she said, punctuating her words with her cane. (I thought I was dead!) "We've heard some words this morning that we've never heard in this tabernacle before." (I knew I was dead!) "But it was good. Wish I'd heard that when I was a girl!" It seems that those most appreciative of my honesty on sexual issues are older adults who grew up with false guilt and unbiblical "preaching" about sexuality.

★ "Talking about sex will make kids want to experiment with it." Most scientific studies reveal that the more talk, the less experimentation. There is something attractive about the hidden and forbidden.

★ "Who's going to teach it?" Probably you. You're the one who bought this book and are reading this chapter. A friend and I have been labeled the "Masters and Johnson" of my denomination merely because no one else was talking or writing about this subject 20 years ago. It's a lot easier to write and speak about other issues. But until more people sense the need for teaching parents how to teach sexual values to their children, you and I are the ones!

4. Set up a committee to work on the series. Include the appropriate supervisors, leaders, directors, youth sponsors, and interested parents.

5. Get the dates on the calendar.

Organize Parents' Meetings

1. Meet with the committee to discuss materials, films, guest speakers.

2. Collect materials.

3. Establish objectives and subjects to be covered. **Learning to Love** suggests these broad subjects:

a.) Contemporary sexual morality and biblical standards

b.) Parental attitudes and responsibilities

c.) Basic anatomy and reproduction

d.) Discussing sex in the home (see previous chapter)

e.) The misuse of sex

4. Establish format: Will the session be films and discussion? Lectures and questions? Open discussion? What about the distribution of books and pamphlets for individual study? If your school, organization, or church isn't ready for a series, this book may meet some of the needs. (Of course, you're buying copies of this book for everyone, right?!) Or you may choose a combination of all of the above.

Conduct the Series

1. Advertise. This may be a great time for those not attending your group or church to discover its relevancy.
2. Have a time of refreshments as a "crowd-breaker."
3. Stress in the first presentation that children want to hear about sex from parents. It's "us or the bus" when it comes to the sex education of most children. (You may want to use appendix A as a resource.)
4. Prepare an evaluation form to determine the strengths and weaknesses in the presentations and program.
5. Encourage your teens to go to their parents for questions about sex. The young people are probably dying to know what Mom and Dad have been talking about in "those meetings."

And encourage Mom and Dad to take their responsibility for sex education seriously. Otherwise their children will think rhythm birth control is having sex while listening to the stereo.

1. Michael R. and Mary Dan Eades, **Protein Power** (New York, New York: Bantam, 1996).
2. Kathleen Stassen Berger, **The Developing Person: Through the Life Span** (New York, New York: Worth Publishers, 1998), 422–424, 497, 500.
3. From **Jim Watkins' Only Hits** compact disk, ©1998, available online at www.jameswatkins.com.
4. Frederick Meeker, "Broken Hearts: The End of 150 Romances," a paper presented at the Western Psychological Association in San Francisco, 1970.
5. For the politically correct police, I'm not referring to those who are vocally challenged!
6. M. Scott Peck, **The Road Less Traveled** (New York, New York: Simon and Schuster, 1978), 84.
7. These five stages were originally defined by Elisabeth Kubler Ross. For more information about them, read her book, **On Death and Dying** (New York, New York: Macmillan, 1969).
8. Terrance D. Olson, **A Report to the Utah State Board of Education on a Federal Family Life Project** (Provo, Utah: AANC, 1985), 3.
9. Donald Joy, **Bonding** (Nappanee, Indiana: Evangel Publishing House, 1997). Provides fascinating reading on this subject.
10. "Boy George" O' Dowd, "Culture Club," **Rolling Stone Online** at http://www.rollingstone.tunes.com
11. Wayne E. Oates, "Counseling the Homosexual Person," **Critical Issues: Homosexuality** (Nashville: The Christian Life Commission of the Southern Baptist Convention, 1989), 13.

12. Ibid.

13. God's Word does have a lot to say about our thought life and moral behavior. Check out these verses for further reading on the subject: Matthew 15:16–20; Mark 7:21; Acts 15:20, 29; 21:5; Romans 12:2; 13:13; 1 Corinthians 5:9; 6:9–20; 10:8; 2 Corinthians 12:21; Galatians 5:19–21; Ephesians 5:3–5; Colossians 3:5; 1 Thessalonians 4:3–6; Hebrews 12:16; 13:4; Jude 7; and Revelation 2:14, 20; 9:21; 21:8; 22:15.

14. Tim Stafford in "Living Together: Experiment in Failure," **Campus Life**, May 1978. Similar results have been documented by Joseph Garza of Georgia State University, Ned Gaylin of the University of Maryland, Jeffery Jacques and Karen Chason of Florida A&M University, and E. Mansell Patterson of the Medical College of Georgia.

15. "Condom Effectiveness Study in Los Angeles Loses Funding," **The Washington Post**, August 10, 1988.

16. "Postabortal Pelvic Infection Associated with Chlamydia Tracomatis and the Influence of Humoral Immunity," Stellan Osser, MD, and Kenneth Persson, MD, **American Journal of Obstetrics and Gynecology**, November 1984, 699–703.

17. Six studies including "Ectopic Pregnancy and Prior Induced Abortion," Ann Aschengrau Levin, et. al., **American Journal of Public Health**, March 1982, 253.

18. Eight studies including "Delayed Reproductive Complications after Induced Abortion," Knut Dalaker, et. al., **Acta Obstet Gynecol Scand**, 1979.

19. Fourteen studies including "A Study on the Effects of Induced Abortion on Subsequent Pregnancy Outcome," Carol Madore, M.A., **American Journal of Obstetrics and Gynecology**, March 19, 1981, 516–521.

20. Two studies including "Oral Contraceptive Use and Early Abortion as Risk Factors for Breast Cancer in Young Women," M. C. Pike, **British Journal: Cancer**, 1981, 72–76.

21. Three studies including "Delayed Reproductive Complications after Induced Abortion," Knut Dalaker, et. al., **Acta Obstet Gynecol Scand**, 1979.

22. Two studies including "Legal Abortion: A Critical Assessment of Its Risks," Stallworthy, et. al., **Lancet**, December 1971, 1245–1249.

23. Ibid.

24. Editorial, "Psychological Sequelae of Therapeutic Abortion," **British Medical Journal**, May 1976, 1239.

25. "The Psychosocial Outcome of Induced Abortion," J. R. Ashton, **British Journal of Obstetrics and Gynecology**, December 1980, 1115–1122.

26. "Psychosocial Sequelae of Therapeutic Abortion in Young Unmarried Women," Judith S. Wallerstein, MSW; **Archives of General Psychiatry**, vol. 27, December 1972.

27. Editorial, "Psychological Sequelae of Therapeutic Abortion," **British Medical Journal**, May 1976, 1239.

28. Walter Trobisch, **I Married You** (San Francisco, California: Harper and Row, 1971), 86.